PROBATIONARY
AMERICANS

D0199318

PROBATIONARY AMERICANS

Contemporary Immigration Policies and the Shaping of Asian American Communities

Edward J. W. Park and John S. W. Park

Routledge

New York • London

Published in 2005 by
Routledge
Taylor & Francis Group
270 Madison Avenue
New York, NY 10016
www.routledge-ny.com

Published in Great Britain by
Routledge
Taylor & Francis Group
2 Park Square
Milton Park, Abingdon
Oxon OX1 4RN U.K.
www.routledge.co.uk

Copyright © 2005 by Taylor and Francis Books, Inc.

Routledge is an imprint of the Taylor and Francis Group.

Printed in the United States of America on acid-free paper.

10 9 8 7 6 5 4 3

All rights reserved. No part of this book may be printed or utilized in any form or by any electronic, mechanical or other means, now known or hereafter invented, including photocopying and recording, or any other information storage or retrieval system, without permission in writing from the publisher.

Library of Congress Cataloging-in-Publication Data

Park, John S. W.
  Probationary Americans : contemporary immigration policies and the shaping of Asian American communities / John S. W. Park and Edward J. W. Park.
     p. cm.
  Includes bibliographical references and index.
  ISBN 0-415-94750-2 (hc : alk. paper)—ISBN 0-415-94751-0 (pb : alk. paper) 1.
United States—Emigration and immigration—Government policy. 2. Asian Americans. I.
Park, Edward J.W. II. Title.
  JV6483.P37 2004
  305.895'073'090511—dc22

                                                            2004010472

Acknowledgments

This project began over dinner, sometime around the time John was finishing his dissertation and Edward was still an assistant professor. Edward was saying how, if the immigration rules passed in 1996 had been passed about two decades ago, there was probably no chance whatsoever that we could have come to the United States. In 1975, our late mother arrived under a family reunification visa sponsored by her older sister, Soo Jin Kim; despite the support she received from her family, Mom and her two boys relied for a time on public assistance programs to make ends meet. (We remember food stamps distinctly, thinking that American money was more colorful than it really was.) Those public assistance programs are no longer available to persons similarly situated, and sponsors of modest means like our aunt are now subject to financial requirements that most could not meet, as well as to financial risks that most would be unwilling to assume.

We witnessed directly some of these dramatic changes to immigration law and policy that we examine in this book. During the last year of John's dissertation, he worked at Van Der Hout and Brigagliano, an immigration law firm based in San Francisco. There, in addition to the new rules governing family reunification, he learned about labor certifications, H-1Bs, national interest waivers, and how to spot an "alien of extraordinary ability." He also saw first hand how powerful information technology firms were recruiting large numbers of immigrants, many from Asia. At the same time, a different team of attorneys at the firm struggled with the new and powerful set of rules governing the "removal" of immigrants convicted of crimes in the United States. In Los Angeles, Edward volunteered as the Director of Research at the Korean Immigrant Workers Advocates in Los Angeles, where he saw the increasing bifurcation of the Korean

American community and the heightened legal and social vulnerability of working-class and poorer immigrants. These experiences at the law firm and at KIWA were invaluable, and this combination of family history, day-to-day work, and community service formed the basic ideas for this book. We would like to thank especially Christine Brigagliano, Roy Hong, and Danny Park for their support.

In 2000, when John finally completed his dissertation in Jurisprudence and Social Policy at the University of California at Berkeley, Michael Omi signed off as one of his advisors. Professor Omi had also been one of Edward's advisors when he had filed his dissertation in the Department of Ethnic Studies in 1993. Professor Omi thus had a major influence on our lives — his theory of racial formation, developed with Howard Winant, obviously shaped much of the theoretical framework for this endeavor. His devotion to his students is legendary, and we owe him our most heartfelt thanks.

During the course of this project, we received excellent criticism and many valuable ideas. We would like to thank receptive audiences at the annual conferences for the Society for the Study of Social Problems, the Association for Asian American Studies, the American Sociological Association, and the Law and Society Association, where portions of this book were presented as conference papers. John also gave talks to students and colleagues in the Department of Sociology and in the Department of Asian American Studies, both at the University of California at Santa Barbara. Edward gave lectures for the Program in Asian American Studies at Arizona State University and at the Asian Pacific American Law and Public Policy Conference at Harvard University. The interest and support generated from these lectures gave us further incentives to push forward.

From the University of California at Santa Barbara, we received grants from the Academic Senate, as well as a Regents' Junior Faculty Fellowship. Both sources were critical for gathering materials for this project, and we are especially grateful to Associate Vice Chancellor Maria Herrera-Sobek for her constant support. We also received financial support from the Rains Academic Research Assistant Program and the Dean's Office of the Bellarmine College of Liberal Arts, both at Loyola Marymount University.

Our first editor at Routledge, Vikram Mukhija, supported this project from its inception, and Karen Wolny and Robert Tempio patiently waited for its completion. Sylvia Wood oversaw the final production process, and Jacquelyn Bergeron facilitated correspondence and other administrative matters for the Press.

At Santa Barbara, Hung Cam Thai, Celine Parrenas Shimizu, Diane Fujino, Xiaojian Zhao, and Douglas Daniels have been wonderful colleagues. Xiaojian Zhao and Douglas Daniels have truly gone out of their way to support John professionally and personally. Howard Winant in Sociology has also been very encouraging and enthusiastic about this and other projects. Venus Nasri and Arlene Phillips have created a most pleasant work environment in John's home department.

At Loyola Marymount University, Kenyon Chan and Fr. Michael Engh, former and current Dean, respectively, of Bellarmine College of Liberal Arts, each provided support and encouragement. Excellent administrative support from Sarah Harkness allowed Edward to redirect precious time and energy from administrative duties to research and writing.

Malisa Lee, Kristyn Kifune, and Kimberly Schreiber provided valuable research assistance at Santa Barbara, as did Kaeleen Ng, Krystle Swaving, and Gilbert Visser at Loyola Marymount.

Finally, we would like to thank our families for their love and devotion, especially during the past four years we've been working on this book together. Edward would like to thank his wife, Reiko Furuta, for her generosity and understanding during the most difficult stages of research and writing, particularly during the many weekends spent ninety miles away in John's office in Santa Barbara. Ben and Hideko Furuta have provided love and encouragement not just for this project, but for all of Edward's personal and professional ventures for the past fifteen years. Matthew and Elise Park provided wonderful distractions.

Gowan Lee, John's better half, waited and waited patiently for him to complete yet another book, one that he kept promising and promising would be done "soon." John is yet again thankful for her patience, faith, and love. Gowan's parents, Hung Ku Lee and Joung Sun Lee, have always been generous, wise, and also very patient. And of course, John would like to thank and acknowledge his own lovely distractions — Zoe, Isabel, and Sophie.

We dedicate this book to the loving memory of our mother, Soo Boon Kim, who came to the United States in 1975 with just three suitcases and two children. We are and always have been truly blessed, but Mom was certainly the greatest blessing of all.

Contents

List of Tables

CHAPTER 1

The Next American Nation

We live in an age of mass migration that is unparalleled in American history. During the last great wave of migration, between 1880 and 1920, about 24 million persons arrived in the United States as immigrants, the vast majority from various parts of Europe. The new wave of migration is no less impressive, perhaps even more so if contemporary trends remain steady. Since 1970, over 21 million persons have settled in the United States as permanent residents, mostly from Mexico, Central America, and Asia. If this decade produces even half the number of immigrants as the last, then the forty years from 1970 to 2010 will have produced the most immigrants to the United States ever. We may not even need the next six years to reach this goal—if one factors in undocumented migrants who have no intention of leaving, then we have most likely exceeded 25 million new immigrants permanently residing in the United States since 1970.

In the past two decades, scholars and public officials have differed widely over whether this current trend is a catastrophe or a blessing, not unlike the generation of scholars and public officials who witnessed the last great wave of migration. In response to the common perception that that migration was indeed a catastrophe, Congress passed a series of rules in the 1910s and 1920s that severely limited migration to the United States for about forty-five years. It was the "tribal twenties," according to the eminent historian John Higham, a time when President Calvin Coolidge said that "America should be kept for the Americans," and everyone knew what he had meant. Politicians complained regularly about "indigestible race," "degenerates," and "aliens ineligible for citizenship." Newspapers and politicians referred to immigrants in less charitable terms. Nationally, of course, the trend toward such incivility to immigrants dated to the time of the Chinese Exclusion Act in 1882, when prominent federal judges referred to Asian immigrants as "vast hordes" for whom "[restricting] further immigration was felt to be necessary to prevent the degradation of white labor, and to preserve to ourselves the inestimable benefits of our Christian civilization."[1]

In our own day, political commentators and polemicists have attacked the latest and largest waves of immigrants in books with alarming titles like *Alien Nation, Invasion, Mexifornia,* and *The Death of the West.* Lately, even liberals writing about immigration and "multiculturalism" use similarly disconcerting titles: the former Democratic governor of Colorado, Richard Lamm, entitled his book, *The Immigration Time Bomb.* Arthur Schlesinger, the noted historian and former special advisor to President Kennedy, titled his work *The Disuniting of America,* and he included there prescriptive ideas about how an increasingly multicultural society needed to achieve a sense of common identity. The only other option was to perish.[2]

Among academics, immigration rules and patterns have inspired a wide range of scholarly contributions from every conceivable field. Economists, sociologists and anthropologists, urban studies scholars, legal scholars, political scientists, political theorists, literary theorists, and historians have all made rich contributions to our understanding of contemporary immigration.[3] Many scholars talk now of "globalization," "flexible citizenship," or the declining significance of national boundaries, while others have pointed out—especially in light of September 11—that citizenship status and national boundaries remain central principles regulating membership and protection.

The heightened level of debate has been matched by a dizzying array of policy changes that have reflected the profound anxiety and conflict over immigration. The Immigration Act of 1965 laid the foundations for our newest wave of migration, but in the last two decades—and especially since 1990—the United States has fundamentally transformed its immigration policies. Most of these changes have been incremental, but the central task of this book is to map these changes and to present them in their entirety, to make an argument about how the principles of the landmark Immigration Act of 1965 no longer dominate American immigration law. In its place, immigration policy is now a complicated system of admissions and removal, of outright privileging of rich over poor, and of assessing in an unprecedented way various levels of "usefulness" to determine immigration status, whether for permanent residents, temporary workers, or guest workers.

In addition to regulating the numbers and types of immigrants who may come or stay, the recent policy changes have in their aggregate moved away from the more liberal principles of the Act of 1965. In one decisive shift, the Act of 1965 had provided for the first race-neutral method for selecting migrants to United States, and consequently, the vast majority of migrants here have since been from non-European countries. We argue that displeasure with the class-based and racial consequences of that reform have driven much of the current policies that embrace immigrants who are "useful," while at the same time excluding and removing those considered "undesirables."

Race and class dimensions characterize contemporary changes in immigration rules and policies: in light of the tremendous advances in transportation and information technology, the highly talented and affluent are now part of a dynamic transnational world characterized by a kinetic "brain circulation" across the boundaries of nation-states.[4] On the other hand, in light of the political anger against poorer immigrants, especially those who come without inspection, nation-states like the United States are asserting new and more physical barriers, in massive coordinated efforts like "Operation Gatekeeper," "Operation Hold the Line," and "Operation Safeguard." More people entered the United States as highly skilled workers in fiscal year 2001 than in any year in American history, but more people also died that year trying to enter the United States illegally than in any other year for which we have records. Those in the first category took jobs as highly paid technical workers, and most came from Asia; those in the second category were trying to find any kind of job, and most came from Mexico, Central America, and Asia. In the fiscal year 2000, the United States deported, excluded, or removed about 185,000 persons, the highest number for any fiscal year in American history.[5] A few thousand persons facing final orders of deportation were refugees who fled Vietnam, Laos, or Cambodia as children—some as young as one year old—to be sent "back" to nations of which they have no memory. Part of the purpose of this book is to give a common context for these types of disparate trends.

THE NEW IMMIGRATION LAW

This book begins in the middle of things, with a general discussion of immigration law that examines the Immigration Act of 1990, the law that reformulated common preference categories for the selection of immigrants and provided new provisions for deportation. The Act of 1990 was both a culmination of modest, earlier reforms and a harbinger of things to come. Subsequent laws would continue to be guided by concerns about the expense of maintaining certain immigrant populations, and the perception that many immigrants were committing crimes or relying disproportionately on public assistance. The Act of 1990 also greatly expanded possibilities for employment-based migration, another trend that subsequent laws embraced in an effort to attract immigrants considered necessary for economic growth in the United States. Here and in other sections throughout the book, we pay special attention to legislative debates about immigration policy, because they best capture the spirit of the new rules, and because they provide a sense of continuity over time.[6] Also, although the federal courts and executive officials have overruled or modified what Congress has done on occasion, most of the rules have remained as the legislators had originally intended. The federal courts, including the United States Supreme Court, have largely deferred to the will of Congress.

After 1990, Congress moved swiftly and dramatically to reduce the costs of immigration. Part II examines how the law came to treat poorer immigrants and poorer prospective immigrants much more harshly. New rules in 1996 marked distances between immigrants and citizens. These rules removed the social safety net for new immigrants, provided powerful means for deporting those who committed even minor offenses, and developed harsher methods for excluding "undesirables," defined primarily in terms of their class position. These rules have been described as "excessive and cruel," chiefly because they have targeted the most vulnerable immigrants. Instead of allowing for the migration of the poor, especially under family reunification provisions, the recent laws have systematically sought to exclude or remove all "persons likely to become a public charge."

In contrast, Part III reviews a set of rules that have provided an even greater expansion of employment-based migration than the Act of 1990. New legislation passed in 1998 and 2000 account for fundamental changes in employment-based migration. Under these laws, more skilled workers have entered the United States than ever before in American history. The vast majority of these persons were admitted as "non-immigrants," persons who in theory are supposed to stay temporarily in areas of the economy that desperately needed them. Yet this set of rules outlines a new regime of immigration that provides a much easier path toward permanent residency and American citizenship for the highly skilled, while providing the federal government a built-in flexibility moderating the entry of these workers.

Taken together, these differing trends in immigration law and policy are a striking reminder of how laws governing migration can powerfully reconfigure economy and society in the United States. They are also poised to reconfigure American race relations, particularly as the very position of Asian Americans in the American racial hierarchy is changing under the new rules. A recurring argument throughout this book is that American policymakers—through separate pieces of legislation in 1990, 1996, 1998, and 2000—have fundamentally altered the system of preferences and exclusions in the immigration law in a way likely to re-shape Asian American communities. In its totality, the law raises disturbing questions about the future of interracial relationships, labor, and citizenship in the United States. The current trajectory of Asian migration should give all of us pause, to think carefully about the kind of society and the set of social and political values that define this nation in the early 21st century.

PART I
Law

CHAPTER 2

Governing Admission to the United States: Basic Themes

IMMIGRATION LAW AS SOCIAL POLICY: SHAPING ECONOMY AND CULTURE

Immigration law in the United States has been shaped by much larger concerns about the type of political community that majorities of Americans have wanted. Immigration rules thus tell us a great deal about the various kinds of utopian visions that American policy makers and voters have shared, both morally and politically. For example, immigration rules have long reserved important economic opportunities for American citizens first and, to the extent that immigrants encroach upon those opportunities, American citizens have demanded restrictive rules. For an extensive period of time, between 1882 and 1965, immigration rules also restricted Asians and other "undesirable races," on the theory that such persons could never assimilate into, or be acceptable within, mainstream American society. In these ways, immigration law has always served as an important set of social policies that described what the United States should look like as a nation-state—free from persons who were economically or culturally threatening, attractive to those who contribute positively, and always mindful of protecting the interests of American citizens first.

Several legal scholars have noted that American immigration law began in colonial times before the United States was a nation-state, when local authorities passed rules intended to stimulate desirable immigrants while,

9

at the same time, excluding undesirables. Colonies, and then the states, attempted to control migration, promising land and tax benefits on the one hand, while passing outright bans on the entry of "convicts," "paupers," or "persons with loathsome diseases" on the other. In the Declaration of Independence, for example, Thomas Jefferson complained that George III "has endeavoured to prevent the population of these States; for that purpose obstructing the Laws for Naturalization of Foreigners; refusing to pass others to encourage their migrations hither, and raising the conditions of new Appropriations of Lands." The American colonists had wanted the freedom to allow European migrants to establish even more settlements, and they accused the King of taking sides with the "merciless Indian savages" whose lands they coveted.[1]

Once the colonies became an independent nation, issues of migration arose immediately and contentiously over slavery. Allowing for the traffic of slaves, and yet hoping it would not last forever, the delegates wrote a tortured sentence to settle a compromise within the constitution itself: "The migration or importation of such persons as any of the states now existing shall think proper to admit, shall not be prohibited by the Congress prior to the year one thousand eight hundred and eight, but a tax or duty may be imposed on such importation, not exceeding ten dollars for each person." As Kenneth Stampp has noted, the slave states wanted the migration of slaves, of course, but no one ever wanted them as citizens, so the compromise reflected a deep-rooted desire—even in the South—to keep Africans out of the United States, and to maintain a racial balance of whites over blacks.[2] The Naturalization Act of 1790 restricted naturalized citizenship to "free white persons only," a principle in law that would last until 1952.

The legal historian Gerald Neuman has argued that most scholars of immigration tended not to pay attention to the state and sometimes federal immigration rules passed from 1776 to 1882, part of what he calls the "lost century" of immigration law. States did exclude—"convicts," "paupers," "persons with contagious diseases," and free blacks—and the federal government passed ideological restrictions through the Alien and Sedition Acts of 1798. After the discovery of Denmark Vesey's conspiracy in 1822, South Carolina required sailors of African descent to remain in jail until their ships disembarked, for example, and the federal government began registering all immigrants in the wake of the French Revolution in an effort to discover and to deport alien radicals.[3]

But the most restrictive pieces of immigration law were passed in the late 19th and early 20th centuries, after a wave of Asian immigrants and then an even greater wave of European peasants and displaced persons settled in major industrial centers. Excellent scholarly monographs by Ronald Takaki, Charles McClain, Sucheng Chan, Lucy Salyer, Andrew Gyory, Robert Lee, and Erika Lee, just to name a few, have given us detailed accounts of the legal, social, and political forces arrayed against Chinese immigration in the late 19th century, culminating in the Chinese Exclusion Act of 1882.[4] This rule was a landmark in American law—the first immigration law that excluded a group of migrants solely on racial criteria. About forty years after this law, however, the Immigration Act of 1924 virtually suspended immigration altogether, further establishing a National Origins System that would persist for the next forty years. The late historian John Higham provided the seminal historical work that covers the period leading to the nativist 1920s, when political leaders in the United States began "closing the gates" to all newcomers, whether from Asia or from Europe.[5]

Between 1882 and 1924, immigration policy in the United States was once again forged from a complex set of political forces, ranging from concerns about the economic position of poor working-class whites to racist, nativist disdain for "unassimilable" peoples. Often, these forces were intertwined, as racist labor unions—rallying for the protection of working-class whites—frequently accused white capitalists of placing their economic interests over the national interests, and going so far as to pollute the United States with barbarian laborers willing to "under-live" whites in the labor market. Hundreds of American workers detested men like Leland Stanford, whom they perceived as selfish industrialists who hired cheap foreign labor. Stanford had once advocated *unrestricted* immigration, but his political opponents, men like Denis Kearney, the leader of the Workingman's Party in the late 19th century, said that American entrepreneurs ought to forgo higher profits in favor of giving opportunities first and foremost to American workers, even if this means excluding immigrants entirely, especially immigrants of "undesirable races."[6] Under that theory, "The Chinese Must Go." Even Stanford himself, in sympathy with his countrymen, eventually abandoned unrestricted migration as a viable social policy, especially as he began to covet public office.

Such ideas have had great success throughout American history, as a generation later, men like Congressman Albert Johnson, the author of numerous anti-immigrant laws in the early 20th century, continued to build their careers on a form of economic nationalism mixed with racism and nativism.[7] By the early 20th century, leading industrialists like Henry Ford had come around to the nativist cause, sponsoring efforts to "Americanize" the foreigners from Europe, while excluding forever the "hordes from Asia."[8] These views formed the cornerstones for the Chinese

Exclusion Acts and the Immigration Acts of 1917, 1921, and 1924, all nativist, all restrictionist, and passed despite purported labor shortages and the protests of leading industrialists.

By the early 20th century, both economic discrimination against immigrants already in place, and new and total barriers against immigration more generally, rose with the same tide, both having the same intent—to preserve opportunities and resources for American citizens first, and to forever discipline immigration law so that it would always serve the interests of native American workers. Speaking about the impending Act of 1924, a delegate for a leading industrial organization conceded the inevitable: "Immigration from, and emigration to countries peopled by races with which inter-marriage gives deteriorated (or 'half breed') and unsatisfactory results—races socially and politically unassimilable—should be permitted by all governments concerned only for commercial purposes."[9] Above all, immigrants were rejected on the grounds that they were no longer useful to the country, and in many cases, they were racialized in ways that framed them as a significant collective harm to the nation's culture. These types of concerns are found throughout the history of American immigration law, and so it should surprise no one when immigration rules in our contemporary period reflect some of these enduring anxieties.

LABOR AND FAMILIES

Several leading scholars have identified the Immigration Act of 1965 as a major shift in American immigration law, a great revision that moved immigration law into a new era characterized by an embracing of a wider range of immigrant groups—including many perceived a generation earlier as racial pariahs—and a confidence born of the nation's ability to provide economic opportunities to newcomers and citizens alike. The Act of 1965 was the first race-neutral immigration law, one that sorted potential immigrants by looking at their existing family connections to persons already in the United States, or by their employability in the labor market. The Act of 1965 was passed in the midst of the Civil Rights Movement, and during a period of economic growth; in such contexts, the Act of 1965 may indeed have embodied a spirit of optimism in the nation, a spirit reflective of renewed commitments to both racial equality and equality of opportunity. This shift did not come without substantial resistance.

Congress did not change immigration policy in any significant way until after World War II, although several rules—the War Brides Acts of 1945 and 1950, the Displaced Persons Acts of 1948 and 1951, and the Internal Security Act of 1950—did provide for selective admissions and exclusions.[10] None of these rules changed the overall structure of immigration law. The Immigration and Nationality Act of 1952 modified existing provisions of the Act of 1924, and provided a thorough, comprehensive template for all contemporary immigration rules. But it preserved the National Origins system codified in Acts of 1917, 1921, and 1924, a system that was designed to maintain the existing racial balance in the United States, even if that meant systemic exclusions against Asians, Africans, Latinos, and Southern and Eastern Europeans.

Offended by the continuation of a system that so blatantly looked at the race of immigrant applicants, President Harry Truman vetoed the Act, but Congress overrode his veto. Three months after the Act had been passed, Truman established a special committee that recommended a year later that the entire immigration law be rewritten, but without the National Origins System.[11] (Twelve years would pass before the System was abolished.) The only race-based liberalization in the Act of 1952 was the one that repealed all race-based barriers to naturalization, following the lead of President Franklin Roosevelt's repeal of Chinese Exclusion in 1943. In other respects, the leading sponsors of the law, Senator Pat McCarran of Nevada and Representative Francis Walter of Pennsylvania, resisted any rule that would change the racial balance of the United States after World War II. A clear majority of Congress supported them in their resistance.

The Act of 1952 would also continue to protect the interests of American workers. Though the Act of 1952 provided for a preference system privileging the admission of "skilled laborers" who were "urgently needed," as well as "temporary workers," neither of these migrant groups was to compete directly with American workers. This system was intended to capture labor shortages in key industries where skilled labor had become increasingly important; it was meant to *supplement* American labor, not to supplant it. Under the new law, employers petitioning the Immigration Service for the arrival of immigrant workers had to petition first to the Department of Labor, which would have to issue a "labor certification" to verify that the immigrant worker "will not adversely affect the wages or working conditions of American workers."[12] This labor certification has remained a ubiquitous feature of the migration process for both immigrants and non-immigrants. The certification process reaffirmed the idea that American workers should enjoy economic opportunities first, before foreigners were offered "their" jobs. Still, most of the Act of 1952 dealt with other avenues of migration, and overall, the Act did not work to stimulate immigration; in 1950, about 250,000 persons came as immigrants; in 1953, 170,000 came as immigrants; and although the numbers rose in subsequent years, immigrants averaged less than 300,000 persons in the fiscal years from 1952 to 1967. The vast majority of immigrants were family-based migrants, not migrants seeking employment.

Orienting immigration policy toward increasing the numbers of skilled laborers did not occur in earnest until ten years after the Act of 1952. In the summer of 1962, the House Judiciary Committee formed a congressional study group to examine immigration policy for seven major purposes, four of which directly involved examining changes in "economic conditions" brought about by migration. The subsequent reports published before the Immigration Act of 1965 recommended a clearly delineated set of preferences for employment-based visas to bring workers with "certain desirable or needed abilities." In the midst of the Space Race and the Cold War, and in light of shortages for medical professionals, the congressional study group identified science and technology workers as among the persons who should benefit most from a liberalized immigration law.

Although labor certifications remained, 54,000 visas would be made available for employment-based migrants; these were divided into two preferences, the first including "members of the professions," or persons with "exceptional ability in the sciences or the arts…[substantially benefiting] prospectively the national economy, cultural interests, or welfare of the United States"; and the second covering persons "capable of performing specified skilled or unskilled labor, not of a temporary or seasonal nature, for which a shortage of employable and willing persons exists in the United States."[13]

Prior to the passage of the law, major labor unions and trade associations insisted on the enforcement and clarification of labor certification standards, so that native workers wouldn't be harmed by the 54,000 immigrants coming for jobs every year. The previous rule gave the Secretary of Labor the authority to block immigrant workers deemed harmful to the interest of American workers; the language said that the Secretary of Labor had the authority to stop the migration of persons "adversely affecting" the position of American workers. The new rule in 1965 began with the presumption that foreign workers were not necessary, then required American employers to prove that foreign workers were in fact necessary. This subtle but important shift marked a major victory for the AFL-CIO, as well as other professional and trade associations. Until the Secretary of Labor agreed with the employer that no foreigner would harm the economic position of an American citizen, the migration of the foreign worker would be blocked.[14] Despite these new burdens, American employers could now cast a wider net to attract talent from across the world. The immediate cohorts of employment-based migrants raised a stir in the years following the Act of 1965: within a few short years, there was talk in Congress of a "brain drain," a large and significant movement of skilled workers from industrial and developing countries into the United States.[15]

The majority of these skilled workers came from Asia. Although by 1980 most Asian immigrants came under family reunification preferences, the sheer number of persons from Asia entering under employment categories was impressive. According to Ronald Takaki, "In 1970, 24 percent of all foreign physicians entering the United States came from the Philippines, far ahead of Canada with eight percent and Britain with six percent." "In 1980 New York City had a concentration of 20 to 25 percent of all Korean-immigrant nurses and doctors," and "the recent Korean immigrants have generally come from the college-educated middle class rather than from the farming and working classes."[16] In a report published in 1993, the National Science Foundation noted that by 1970, foreign students from Asian countries far surpassed students from European countries in their enrollment in engineering schools in the United States, a trend that has continued to this day. Moreover, foreign doctoral students from Asia were much more likely to stay in the United States than their peers from other parts of the world.[17] Taken together, Asians migrated in very large numbers under the employment provisions of the Act of 1965—as a group, they were profoundly different from previous waves of Asian migrants, and in fact, their class position and educational training made them the most affluent, highly skilled migrants in American history. American newspapers and other media sources began describing Asian Americans as a "model minority," in most instances without alluding to the earlier virulent, racist characterizations of Asian immigrants that for over eight decades justified their systemic exclusion in American immigration law.[18]

RESTRICTING ENTRY TO THE POOR: THE IMMIGRATION ACTS OF 1965, 1986, AND 1990

Many historical accounts of the Act of 1965 have portrayed the rule as a truly liberal turn in American immigration law, but contrary to this view, several aspects of the law were overtly restrictionist, particularly toward poorer laborers and settlers from Mexico, Central America, and South America.[19] Under a "Good Neighbor" policy, the southern border of the United States had been porous—largely unpoliced—and large numbers of persons throughout the Western Hemisphere migrated into the southern border states both before and after World War II. During the War, when workers were in short supply, immigration officials and agricultural growers in the Southwest actively procured laborers from south of the border, often in exploitative arrangements.[20]

But like previous generations of immigrants, these migrants faced increasing hostility, as well as calls to either regulate or restrict their arrival. The Act of 1965 responded to these calls by providing for no more than 120,000 visas per year for persons in the Western Hemisphere, despite the likelihood that this would create backlogs in the countries affected. It did not seem to matter—Congress had heard evidence that migrants from the Western Hemisphere were generally poor, unskilled, and non-white. In 1976, after reviewing reports of "considerable hardship" to immigrants in the Western Hemisphere, mainly from Mexico, the rule was amended such that each country in the Western Hemisphere could send up to 20,000 immigrants per year, thus alleviating some of the backlog in some countries; however, the overall ceiling for the Western Hemisphere remained the same, at 120,000 visas, compared to 170,000 visas for countries in the Eastern Hemisphere.

Only in 1978 did Congress abolish the differentials between Western and Eastern, in favor of a worldwide limit of 20,000 persons per country per year. Despite that development, overall migration from countries most proximate to the United States—especially Mexico—changed after the Act of 1965. Moving back and forth across the border had been a rather mundane and common activity for many Mexican citizens, and even some Americans. That southern border was stiffening, and it would stiffen even further when Congress passed the Immigration Reform and Control Act in 1986.

Fundamentally, the Act of 1986 was passed because it became increasingly obvious that this pattern of moving back and forth across the border for employment purposes had simply not ended with the new restrictions. Supported most ardently by Senator Alan Simpson, the Republican from Wyoming, the Act of 1986 provided for a novel set of seemingly contradictory policies toward "undocumented aliens," persons entering without inspection, mostly from the southern border. For some persons who had been in the United States illegally for several years, including agricultural workers, the Act of 1986 legalized their status: they could petition for permanent resident status without fearing deportation. Under these provisions, an unexpectedly high number of persons—some 2.7 million—adjusted to permanent residency. The Act of 1986 did, though, include special provisions to prevent the entry of similarly situated persons in the American labor market: employers in the United States now had to take affirmative steps to verify that the persons they were hiring did not come to the United States illegally. To increase the likelihood of compliance, and to deter further illegal entries, the Act of 1986 levied sanctions against American companies that knowingly hired undocumented workers.[21]

The employer penalties in the Act of 1986 did have analogs in the past, but the Supreme Court had been reluctant to allow the *federal* government the power to punish American citizens for hiring certain classes of immigrants, even if such punishment followed from business relationships with immigrants. For instance, in a case in 1909, the Court had considered a congressional statute passed in 1907, which in part said that any citizen procuring or importing an alien woman for purposes of prostitution shall be "guilty of a felony, and on conviction thereof be imprisoned not more than five years and pay a fine of not more than five thousand dollars." The prostitute herself would be deported.[22]

Justice David Brewer had said that such a rule unduly infringed on the police powers of the state over citizens—states, not the federal government, should punish persons for trafficking in prostitution, as they did with other regulations for health, safety, and welfare. Brewer thought it unwise to allow the federal government such encroachment in all such dealings between citizens and foreigners: "Jurisdiction over such an offense comes within the accepted definition of the police power. Speaking generally, that power is reserved to the States, for there is in the Constitution no grant thereof to Congress."[23] Without such restraint, "an immense body of legislation, which heretofore has been recognized as peculiarly within the jurisdiction of the States, may be taken by Congress away from them. ... Then we should be brought face to face with such a change in the internal conditions of this country as was never dreamed of by the framers of the Constitution."[24] Under this reasoning, the Court had rejected the idea that Congress could punish American *citizens* as a way to control immigration problems. But ever since the idea was resurrected in the Act of 1986, contemporary federal courts have upheld these penalties against constitutional challenges.[25]

Despite the fact that many American employers were ignoring the prohibition of the Act of 1986, the Immigration Act of 1990 redoubled efforts to keep undocumented aliens out of the country. Almost every fine and penalty against employers hiring or procuring illegal aliens was increased, and citizens could be fined for a broader range of aiding and abetting activities, including document fraud. Also, an entire section of the Act of 1990 dealt with increased measures to stiffen the southern border, including an increase in the total number of Border Patrol agents and monies "for the repair, maintenance, or construction on the United States border, in areas experiencing high levels of apprehensions of illegal aliens, of structures to deter illegal entry into the United States."[26] If the Act of 1965 provided for numerical formulas as a way to regulate the migration of poorer persons across the southern border, the Act of 1990 provided for fences, moats, and other physical barriers that could literally stretch across miles of land and into the sea. The Act of 1990 continued in this way the trend of limiting access to the United States for persons who were likely to be poor.

FAMILY REUNIFICATION IN THE IMMIGRATION ACT OF 1990

Though it retained most of the criteria for admitting persons into the United States, the Immigration Act of 1990 reframed the structure of immigration rules. Since the Immigration Act of 1990, there have been four general ways to obtain permanent resident status in the United States. Under two avenues, an immigrant may self-petition for resident status, either as a refugee, asylee, or a "diversity immigrant"; under the other two avenues, an immigrant must typically rely on someone already settled in the United States, either for family reunification or for employment. These last two avenues have accounted for the vast majority of permanent residents, and so we deal with them first.

The Immigration Act of 1990 was originally intended to make immigration rules less complicated and byzantine, but as we shall see, this worked only to a limited extent. Immigration rules have been and continue to be rather complex, perhaps less so than only the federal tax code.[27] Prior to the changes in 1990, American immigration laws had six general preferences, four for family relationships and two for employment, in addition to a "non-preference" category that had never been used since 1978. In some ways, the Act of 1990 split and defined family and employment preferences more clearly, but not without convoluted math and some counterintuitive logic.

This was especially evident for the immigrant visas based upon family relationships. The visas for family reunification have been the most commonly issued immigrant visas since World War II, and they became a permanent feature of the law when so many American men from that war married and had children with women abroad, especially from Europe. The War Brides Act of 1948 and variants thereafter have given priority to American citizens seeking to reunite with their immediate family members in the United States. These "family members" did include and continue to include the newly wedded spouses of American citizens: from 1950 to 1989, for example, roughly 90,000 Korean women entered the United States as foreign brides, the vast majority having married American servicemen.[28]

The law gave support to the principle of family unity, but in the actual implementation of this simple principle, the system of rules became bizarre and multilayered. In theory, all American citizens and permanent residents have the right to petition for the entry of immediate family members, and there is no numerical quota limiting the reunion of American citizens with their spouses, children, and parents. Of course, all of the terms—"child," "spouse," and "parent"—have been heavily litigated, and some defined by statute, but the essence of the rule has been the same for over fifty years. American citizens are in a much better position to petition for family reunification than permanent residents, and for permanent residents, one key incentive to become naturalized American citizens has been this ability to petition for "immediate family" unrestrained by quotas and other limits. Under the Immigration Act of 1990, all family-sponsored visas are capped at roughly 480,000 per year. Whatever family-sponsored visas are unused by immediate family members of American citizens are apportioned according to the preference system outlined below.

These other family reunification categories are divided into four general preferences. The first preference is for unmarried sons and daughters of American citizens—if they were younger than 21, they could have entered as "immediate family," so this first preference was obviously intended to capture the older children of American citizens. Still, despite the fact that they are technically "immediate family," their total visas are capped at 23,400 persons per year. The second preference accounts for *at least* 114,200 visas per year, reserved for the spouses and unmarried children of permanent residents. The third preference covers the married children of American citizens, which is capped at 23,400. The fourth preference covers the siblings of American citizens, capped at 65,000 visas per year.[29]

Altogether, the combination of ceilings and floors comes to exactly 226,000 visas for persons in these four categories that *must be available* per year. To reduce backlogs in some categories (particularly the second preference), unused visas in one category can be used by persons in other categories, visas unused in one year can carry over into another, and visas that couldn't be issued one year may become available in the subsequent year. The 480,000 total for all persons entering under family reunification visas is a "pierceable cap, with a floor"; that is, if 300,000 people have entered in a given year as immediate relatives of American citizens, 180,000 can enter under the four preferences, *but* in the subsequent year, since 226,000 people must enter under the four preferences (which must be set aside) per year, the cap can be "pierced"—in addition to the 226,000 persons in the second year, another 46,000 visas can be added, distributed to the categories that have the longest queues.

The explanation for this "cap that can be pierced," year after year, as opposed to a real, enforceable cap every year, only makes sense if one sees the tremendous backlogs that tend to develop under the four preferences, as well as the priority given to family reunification within nuclear families. In practice, and in most years, whenever the numbers of admissions for immediate family members of American citizens declines, the unused visas up to 480,000 have been diverted to the second preference category, the most impacted of the family preferences and the one reserved for spouses and children. The Act of 1990 essentially positioned the spouses and children of permanent residents in a privileged position relative to the first preference category, which makes some of us wonder why the first preference isn't the second preference and vice versa. This may seem hopelessly confusing, and many have criticized this system as needlessly complex. Perhaps the only benefit is psychological—the nation fears an unlimited ceiling of immigrants, even for family reunification, but it doesn't want this ceiling to be a *fixed* ceiling. Despite regular calls to eliminate this confusing and complex system—consisting of so much strange math—the system has survived for some time now. Instead of setting clearer, quantitative limits, Congress has in recent years opted for policies that set qualitative and financial criteria applicable for all persons seeking family reunification.

The Act of 1990 did place discrete limits on the number of persons that could come from any one country. The old math was simpler: before the Act of 1990, no more than 20,000 persons could come as immigrants from any one country. Now, "the combined family-sponsored and employment-based immigrants from a single country in a given fiscal year cannot exceed 7% of the combined family and employment worldwide limit…unless such a per-country limitation would cause worldwide visas to go unused."[30] More simply, there are 480,000 family reunification visas and 140,000 employment-based visas per year; in any given year, no country can send more than 7% of 620,000 (the sum of 480,000 and 140,000), which works out to 43,400 visas per country, or 33,600 family-based visas and 9,800 employment-based visas, provided all categories are apportioned perfectly, which of course they never are. Again, this per-country limit is a "pierceable cap"—if fewer than 480,000 visas are necessary to fulfill all the demand for family reunification in a given year, *or* if fewer than 140,000 visas are enough to fulfill the demand for employment-based visas, a single country can send more than 43,400 immigrants. The cap is also pierceable because some immigrants, namely the immediate family members of American citizens and permanent residents (except for their adult children), are not charged against the cap, which again emphasized the reunification of families.

As complex as this system was, the Act of 1990 represented a victory of sorts for immigrant advocates who wished to retain an underlying commitment to family reunification, a commitment that had been part of the immigration law since 1965. In the 1980s, influential lawmakers had questioned whether the United States should continue to privilege family reunification over economic concerns—whether the United States should use immigration policy to grow the economy and to attract skilled workers, and not necessarily to allow brothers and sisters or distant relatives to reunite in this country.[31] By 1992 and 1993, record numbers of immigrants were coming to the United States, a clear majority entering under family reunification provisions retained in the Act of 1990. By 1993, a growing number of legislators were concerned that these levels of immigration were just too high; in California, voters were told in a bitter political campaign that immigrants overall, and undocumented aliens especially, were too dependent upon welfare and other forms of public assistance.[32] In 1994, California voters unanimously passed Proposition 187, a draconian immigration rule that cut off all non-emergency medical care to undocumented aliens, as well as denying undocumented students access to the state's public schools.

For many observers, this turn represented a backlash against existing immigration policies, a backlash based upon resentment at existing rules that permitted the migration of persons "likely to be poor," even if they arrived for family reunification. Critics argued that immigration law had always been concerned, and always should be concerned, with economic consequences first, and they called for reforms to realign the law in that direction.[33] Federal rules in 1996 would severely curtail social services to legal immigrants, and these rules would discourage or even disqualify poorer families from ever seeking family reunification.

EMPLOYMENT-BASED IMMIGRATION IN THE IMMIGRATION ACT OF 1990

Over the same period, between 1952 and 1994, the legal paths into the United States for immigrants with skills and capital improved considerably. The Immigration Act of 1990 itself raised the ceiling for employment-based visas, from 54,000 to 140,000 per year, and provided the majority of these visas to persons who were highly skilled and otherwise useful, even creating four new categories of entry that were distinctly *not* egalitarian. The Act of 1990 provided for five broad categories for the distribution of employment-based immigration, apportioned in a familiar preference system described below.

First preference immigrants were defined as "priority workers," subdivided into three categories: "aliens of extraordinary ability"; "outstanding professors and researchers"; and "multinational executives and managers." First preference immigrant visas were "not to exceed 40,000" per fiscal year.

The second preference covered "professionals holding advanced degrees," or persons who have the equivalent of advanced degrees, or persons with "exceptional ability in the sciences, arts, or business," and who will "substantially benefit prospectively the national economy, cultural or educational interests, or welfare of the United States." Second preference immigrant visas were "not to exceed 40,000" per fiscal year. In addition, employers seeking to hire immigrant workers under the second preference had to obtain a labor certification, although this could be waived by the Attorney General if such a waiver was in the "national interest."

Third preference immigrants covered three types of workers: "skilled workers," defined as "qualified immigrants who are capable, at the time of petitioning for classification under this paragraph, of performing skilled labor (requiring at least 2 years training or experience), not of a temporary or seasonal nature, for which qualified workers are not available in the United States"; "professionals," persons "who hold baccalaureate degrees and who are members of the professions"; and "other workers," "[capable] of performing unskilled labor, not of a temporary or seasonal nature, for which qualified workers are not available in the United States." This last subcategory can have no more than 10,000 of the 40,000 visas allotted to the third preference. For all immigrants under the third preference, a labor certification was required without exception.

The fourth preference included "special immigrants," a catchall category that in previous legislation included everyone from "religious workers" to "former long-term employees of the United States government." No more than 10,000 visas were to be apportioned for persons in the fourth preference.

Finally, the fifth preference was labeled "employment creation," but it is more commonly known as the "one million dollar visa." Any investor whose efforts can create ten full-time jobs in the American economy gets one of these exceptional visas, and although the figure was originally set at $1 million, the Act of 1990 gave the Attorney General discretion to raise this amount in some areas or lower it in others, depending upon the needs of different parts of the country where the immigrant wished to settle. The basic idea was that if an immigrant's investment can directly benefit American workers, then he or she gets to stay permanently. Up to 10,000 persons could gain permanent resident status in this way. Persons under the fifth preference were given a status that was "conditional," meaning that the status could be revoked if the investment turned out to be fraudulent or otherwise did not materialize.[34]

Altogether, the arrangement of the five preferences was a major victory for scholars and politicians who had long advocated the use of immigration rules for economic purposes. The increase in the overall cap represented about a 160% increase in the total numbers of persons coming as employment-based immigrants. In theory, no one could come without a job offer, or at least an extremely high likelihood of becoming employed almost immediately—persons with "extraordinary ability" or "outstanding" were just the type of people to get multiple job offers. Furthermore, as a compromise with American labor groups, the Acts of 1965, 1986, and 1990 were phrased such that immigrant workers arriving in the United States would not compete with American workers, for if such a possibility existed, their employers would never have received labor certifications from the Secretary of Labor to employ them.

The requirements for labor certification were quite extensive. Any employer hiring a foreigner had to have to taken affirmative steps to hire an American citizen first: they must have advertised in newspapers and in trade publications the position that the foreigner was about to take, in such a manner that American citizens interested in the position would have seen these advertisements; they must have interviewed all American citizens interested in the position, even though some may have appeared obviously unqualified; they must have offered to all persons the same wage, whether American or foreign; and they must accept the help of state officers and agencies in finding an American worker, since the first step in labor certification requires reporting the vacancy in question to a state job service agency.

The Act of 1990 also gave broad discretion to the INS to review all employment-related visas, so that even if an employer had labor certification, the Service was still entitled to investigate whether the immigrant employee was indeed qualified, or whether the employer was a legitimate company capable of paying the prevailing wage stated in the labor certification. To ascertain these facts, the Service could request full disclosure of financial documents, a report on the industry in which the employer was engaged, and other formal statements about the employer and the employee. Any instance of fraud or misrepresentation could leave the employer subject to civil and criminal penalties. All of this meant that any employer petitioning for an immigrant in the second or third preference, as well as any immigrant petitioning for the million dollar visa, was subject to a bureaucratic and financial examination roughly equivalent to an

IRS audit. Even many of the penalties were the same: the IRS can take one's airplane if it was used to evade taxes; the INS can also take the company jet if it was used to transport second-preference employment-based immigrants before the proper labor certifications were processed.[35] Reviewing the language of the law, corporate sponsors would conclude that it would just be easier, and generally safer, to hire an American citizen.

DIVERSITY AND ANTI-DIVERSITY IN THE IMMIGRATION ACT OF 1990

Everyone studying immigration trends knew that the migratory flows that had developed under the Act of 1965 had been uneven—far more persons were coming from Asia and Latin America than from anywhere else. According to Stephen Legomsky, a leading scholar of immigration law, "Congress [was] quite disturbed by these patterns." In 1988, Congress created a special OP-1 visa created for aliens from "under-represented countries," countries that had used fewer than 25% of their maximum number of visas in that year. Several legislators had countries like Ireland in mind when they considered this rule, as such European countries were much more likely than Asian countries to fit these criteria. Legomsky and others claimed that the "diversity visas," which were created in the Act of 1990 and would be available by 1994, were in fact "anti-diversity" visas, since the majority of persons benefiting from this program would come from Europe, "although Africa also appear[ed] likely to receive a substantial share."[36] One scholar claimed that this was the equivalent of an immigration policy "[operating] as an affirmative action program for white immigrants."[37]

Whether legislators intended to or not, the diversity lottery in recent years has produced roughly even numbers of immigrants from Europe and Africa, as well as a significant fraction from countries in Asia, including Bangladesh, Nepal, and even Taiwan. Initially, most of the beneficiaries were in fact Europeans, although most of them have also been from Eastern and Southern Europe—Albania, Lithuania, Bulgaria, Poland, Romania, Russia, and the Ukraine—hardly places thought to be desirable sources of American immigration throughout American history. But the balance toward Europe has been less severe in recent years. In the fiscal year 2001, for example, about 18,000 persons from Europe, about 6,000 from Asia, and about 15,000 from Africa were admitted under this visa. Certain countries send many winners: the biggest winners in the diversity lottery in 2003, for example, were Nigerians.[38]

More importantly, though, the immigrants entering under the DV visa must meet certain threshold requirements that limit the likelihood that they will become a public charge. First, applicants to the lottery must prove one of the following: that they "completed a high school education," or that they have "two years of experience within the past five years in an occupation that requires at least two years of training or experience." The visa thus was structured to provide diversity in terms of national origin, but not necessarily in terms of class background—most of the very poor would be disqualified. Nevertheless, the visa has become increasingly popular, and so the odds of "winning" have grown more remote: 13 million applications were filed in 2000, and 8.7 million in 2001.[39] Originally, 55,000 visas were to be available each year, but that number has since been reduced to 50,000 through subsequent legislation, further reducing the chances of success.[40]

As of this writing, the United States Department of State maintains a website for prospective lottery participants that lists the requirements for applying for this visa. At the outset, the site lists the countries that are ineligible for the lottery, and they include Canada, mainland China, Colombia, India, Haiti, the Dominican Republic, Jamaica, Mexico, Pakistan, the Philippines, South Korea, the United Kingdom, and Vietnam. As one can easily see, the majority of these countries are in the Caribbean, Latin America, or Asia. One imagines a person from Haiti or from the Philippines looking at this website and getting the impression that the United States is saying in a not-so-subtle way that there are already too many of you.

Basic Themes and Concepts in Immigration Admissions

Since 1990, all immigrants to the United States have obtained permanent residency through one of the immigrant visas created by the Act of 1990. As a massive reworking of American immigration rules, the Act of 1990 strengthened restrictions against poorer migrants, particularly from the Western Hemisphere, while at the same time providing for a much larger pool of skilled laborers to the enter the United States. On the one hand, the Act of 1990 carried over trends in the Acts of 1965 and 1986, and created new barriers for poor laborers—physical barriers and increased border patrols authorized by the Act of 1990 have contributed to what several scholars have called the "militarization" of the southern border. On the other, the Act of 1990 increased the total number of immigrants coming under employment categories by about 160%. Even though persons immigrating for employment purposes did face bureaucratic hurdles designed to protect American workers, this method of entry into the United States was obviously and dramatically broadened.

The Act of 1990 was thus a remarkable shift toward an aggressive, employment-based orientation to the immigration law. Moreover, despite concerns that family reunification visas were allowing too many poorer families to enter, the Act of 1990 did not change the basic rules governing family reunification. That it failed to encompass such changes—to make family reunification more difficult—immediately inspired new reforms to again discourage persons not likely to contribute directly to the economy of the United States.

CHAPTER 3

Exclusion, Deportation, and Refugee Admissions

THE UNDESIRABLES: EXCLUSION UNDER THE IMMIGRATION ACT OF 1990

Whether prospective immigrants intended to arrive under a family reunification visa or under an employment-based visa, they had to show that they did not fall within one of the several grounds for exclusion. There were many reasons why persons could not immigrate to the United States: before the Act of 1990, there were more than thirty specific reasons. The Act of 1990 listed nine, which were now listed under amended §212 of the Immigration and Nationality Act.[1] Most of the grounds for exclusion can be dealt with quickly here. All are as illuminating as the grounds for immigration admissions, for they tell us a great deal about the type of persons considered deviant in American society. More importantly, they help us see a recurring theme: persons conceived as burdensome economically should not be admitted.

In both political rhetoric and in practice, health-related grounds for exclusion date to the Chinese Exclusion period, when the Chinese were often described as carriers of exotic diseases.[2] Since that era, immigration rules have reflected legitimate public health concerns as well as the not-so-legitimate concerns of racist, nativists, and proponents of various eugenics movements. Immigration rules have restricted the "mentally unfit" and "persons with physical disorders"—indeed, entire classes and nationalities were sometimes conceived as a form of pollution, thus inspiring rules that barred entire regions and continents.[3] For American policy-makers in the early 20th century, most of the deviant types of humanity came from southern and eastern Europe, or they were Jews, Africans, and Asians. As we have noted, racial criteria in the immigration law until 1952 assumed that certain peoples were biologically and intellectually unfit for American citizenship. There were other types of persons who were similarly unfit: until the Act of 1990, persons with psychopathic personalities were excluded under this category, and this included homosexuals.[4] In 1990, Congress no longer barred homosexuals, but it did exclude persons infected with the HIV virus, which was described in the law as "the etiologic agent for acquired immune deficiency syndrome."

The second ground for exclusion in the Act of 1990 concerned prior criminal activity—any alien who has been convicted of crimes involving "moral turpitude" or a similar serious offense is barred from entry. This category also mentioned drug traffickers and prostitutes—the former a category added recently to the list of excludable aliens, and the latter a category that dates back to one of the first federal immigration rules in American history, the Page Law of 1875, which barred the entry of "lewd and debauched women." The principle of excluding anyone who has a prior criminal conviction has remained in the law ever since.

If the Attorney General or the consular officer issuing a visa abroad has reasonable grounds to think that an alien may pose a threat to the American government, either through espionage, sabotage, or any other unlawful means, that alien may be excluded under the third general category. In principle, this ground for exclusion dates to the first federal immigration rules ever, the Alien and Sedition Acts of 1798, and it was reiterated in 1918 in a law barring "subversives," as well as in broader rules like the Internal Security Act of 1950. The original statutes—some dating to the early 20th century—defined "terrorist activities" to include any unlawful act "under the laws of the place where it was committed," and it also excluded persons who were members of, or associated with, any "individual, organization, or government" sponsoring terrorist activities. Revisions since then included anyone affiliated with a communist organization, anyone who participated in the Nazi government in the persecution or murder of others, and anyone who participated in genocide.[5]

Still, this category has not been without controversy or irony. Since the founding of Israel as a nation-state, the Palestinian Liberation Organization and all of its members have been defined as terrorists. Several American presidents have insisted that even under the white racist South African government, Nelson Mandela and his associates in the African National Congress were all terrorists, too. However, this was how Nelson

Mandela described his visit to the United States in June of 1990: "I had read about New York City when I was a young man, and finally to see it from the bottom of its great glass-and-concrete canyons while millions upon millions of pieces of ticker tape came floating down was a breathtaking experience. It was reported that as many as a million people personally witnessed our procession through the city."[6] Mr. Mandela had been released from a South African prison—where he had been forced to spend twenty-seven years for conspiracy and treason—just four months before this visit.

The fifth ground of exclusion generally concerns labor certification requirements dealt with in other sections of the Immigration and Nationality Act, specifically those dealing with immigrant-based employment visas. The fifth ground is thus mostly redundant: any alien who needs labor certification to work but does not have it is excludable.

The sixth ground for exclusion concerns illegal immigrants, this rule saying specifically that they can be excluded if they were not successfully excluded the first time. The length of their illegal stay is immaterial for purposes of this section—even if undocumented aliens have lived in the United States for many, many years, they are "excluded," not "deported," an important distinction in the law since "exclusion" commonly triggers a lower set of procedural safeguards than "deportation." Moreover, under this section, anyone who was discovered to be illegally present, then was deported, is excludable for up to a year. Other similar types of persons are excludable here: anyone who is a stowaway aboard a vessel, anyone who smuggles others into the country, and anyone who forges documents for the purpose of entering the country.

Among all persons seeking admission into the United States, anyone who doesn't have the proper documents is excludable under the seventh ground for exclusion. This applies to anyone seeking entry, even tourists, and in recent years, the penalties and inconveniences for having improper documents can be considerable.[7]

Anyone who isn't permanently eligible for American citizenship is excludable under the eighth ground. From 1882 until 1943, this general principle applied to Asians, all of whom were deemed by various statutes and court decisions "aliens ineligible for citizenship." Now this category covers people who cannot be naturalized for a variety of reasons, but mostly applies to persons with past criminal records or very bad "moral character." This category also includes "draft evaders," an addition that dates back to the Vietnam War, when so many young men were fleeing to Canada to avoid the draft.

The ninth ground is a catchall category: it names polygamists, child abductors, and persons who depend on anyone who is excludable or deportable. Of the class of persons included in this category, the last is most interesting. If, for example, Edward is excludable and John depends on him for "protection and guardianship," John is excludable, too. A reading of this rule would suggest that it is best not to rely upon anyone facing exclusion or deportation.

Persons Likely to Become a Public Charge

The fourth ground for exclusion has always been one of the most brief, and yet it has analogs dating back into the eighteenth century, before federal immigration rules and before the establishment of the United States. In recent years, the exclusion of persons "likely to become a public charge" has received renewed attention in the law, and so we pay special attention to it here. The concept itself has a very long history: colonial governments—following the lead of the mother country—established rules to keep out paupers and beggars, even those from the mother country.[8] Before the Civil War, various states in the North prohibited the migration and settlement of persons of African descent, again under the theory that they would not only cause social disruptions, but economic ones as well.[9] Some form of the public charge provision has remained in American law since then, both in early state rules and in federal rules dating to the late 19th century. The General Immigration Law of 1882, passed three months after the Chinese Exclusion Act, "banned" persons who could not support themselves. The public charge provision appeared throughout legislation in the 20th century. Until recently, it was but one sentence: "Any alien who, in the opinion of the consular officer at the time of the application for a visa, or in the opinion of the Attorney General at the time of the application for admission or adjustment of status, is likely at any time to become a public charge is excludable."

Since 1952, because of the difficulty in obtaining employment-based visas, immigrants coming under these categories were rarely ever denied entry under the public charge exclusion. But persons coming under other categories, particularly for family reunification, did have to show that they were either able to work or could rely on another for support. An interesting case in 1957 revealed some of the methods used by government officials to deal with the public charge requirement. Consular officials and officers of the State Department had devised an affidavit of support, a notarized statement that "read like the terms of a contract," with analogs to similar regulations developed during the Chinese Exclusion era and in the Immigration Act of 1924. Anyone petitioning for an immigrant who appeared poor to an immigration official had to attest that they would "receive, maintain, [and] support the aliens after their immigration to the United States, and hereby assume such obligations guaranteeing that none of them will at any time become public charges upon any community in the United States." In some instances, petitioning relatives had to post a special bond in case their relatives ever did become a public charge.[10]

The state of California sued an uncle and aunt, Mr. and Mrs. Renel, to recover charges incurred by an immigrant nephew, Jevrum Karijo, who had become a ward of the state from 1951 to 1955. The facts were sad: "He appear[ed] to have been employed in New York City by his uncle and others for approximately two and a half years following his entry. It was not until August of 1950 that it became necessary to receive him as a psychiatric patient in Bellevue Hospital in the city of New York." Karijo's condition worsened, and he drifted. "Although for a time the defendants, naturalized citizens of the United States, and husband and wife, the wife being the aunt of said immigrant, helped to support him, they ultimately abandoned him to the public authorities and he became an inmate of various public institutions in California."[11] The state of California sued Mr. and Mrs. Renel to recover $4,721, a considerable amount in 1957, since the aunt and uncle had indeed signed an affidavit of support in 1948, the year that their nephew entered the country.

The decision of the City Court in New York relied heavily on the statements of government officials made in other contexts, particularly with regard to a set of refugee laws passed in the late 1940s and early 1950s, including the Displaced Persons Act of 1948 and the Refugee Relief Act of 1953. The City Court noted that during the discussions over these rules, which were intended to relieve enormous refugee problems in Europe, the Commissioner of Immigration as well as legislative study groups phrased the affidavit of support not as a strict contract, but as "a serious moral obligation ... undertaken by the affiant." Congress had not provided clear statutory authorization for the enforcement of affidavits, and although it had provided for the posting of a "public charge bond," the term "affidavit of support" did not appear in any federal statute.

In the absence of this explicit grant of authority from Congress, the City Court reasoned, consular officials did not have the right to require a strict contract between the federal government and the person sponsoring the immigrant beneficiary. The affidavit must thus remain a "moral obligation," not a legally binding one. "If an enforceable legal obligation were contemplated by the statute, it is reasonable to suppose that it would have well-defined limitations concerning amount, duration, and other conditions." Otherwise, it could be catastrophic for the petitioning sponsor: "It is easy to conceive of a situation in which an immigrant might incur medical or other expenses of an extraordinary nature and the liability upon the sponsor might be so great as to be disastrous. If there is such a legal liability, a statute would probably confine it within a reasonable area."[12] The Supreme Court of New York subsequently upheld this decision.[13]

The precedent in *Renel* appeared and prevailed in other cases, in a Michigan case where the immigrant beneficiary required hospital care in 1959, and in a California case where the beneficiary required "medical and hospital services" in San Diego in 1969.[14] In both cases, the state courts ruled that federal statutes did not authorize a contract binding upon the affiant to support an immigrant beneficiary. In the second case, the Court of Appeals in California added reasons suggesting that even if an affidavit of support were in fact a contract, it was not a good idea, because it rendered liability to the petitioning relative or sponsor for acts beyond their control:

> [The] alien is not a party to the alleged contract; is not obligated to do anything which would prevent his becoming a public charge; in nowise is subject to the control of the sponsor; may refuse employment offered him by the sponsor; may neglect his health to the extent he contracts a disabling disease; and in a variety of other ways may so conduct himself that he will become a public charge.[15]

The Court of Appeals could have asked this as a rhetorical question: should a petitioner of an alien be liable for all public benefits consumed by that alien if that person—through no fault of the petitioner—engages in behavior that increases his likelihood of becoming indigent? The Court in California had answered no. Recent legislation would suggest a different answer.

In general, though, this concern with the economic impact of poorer immigrants is reflected in more than half of the qualitative grounds for exclusion. Contagious migrants and otherwise sick immigrants are likely to consume expensive medical services, for example, and since cases like *Renel*, "persons likely to become a public charge" are by definition most likely to depend upon local, state, and federal governments for services when their own relatives cannot support them. In fact, a case like *Renel* helps us see this relationship more clearly: if Jevrum Kajiro's psychological problems had been manifest at the time of his entry, he would have been excluded on health-related grounds. Indeed, the incentive to find and exclude such "costly immigrants" have only increased in recent years, if only because government-sponsored welfare programs since the New Deal have created a kind of "new property" in the form of access to public benefits and other public income transfers.[16] The federal courts, including the United States Supreme Court, have said in numerous instances that state and federal governments may not deny immigrants various forms of public services, even those who entered unlawfully.[17]

Other categories of excludable aliens raise similar issues. The exclusion of criminal aliens, for example, might best be seen not just as a way to keep bad people out of the United States, but to avoid the cost of having to deal with them in a criminal justice system that is as strained and increasingly expensive as the social welfare system. Ironically, by breaking the criminal law, immigrants can for a time share the same status as any native-born American: criminal aliens have a right to an attorney, they have a right to a speedy trial, they have a right to a jury of their peers, they have a right to remain silent and a right against self-incrimination, they have a right to be free from cruel and unusual punishment, and so on. All these legal protections can be costly. Moreover, it is just as expensive to imprison an immigrant in a federal or state facility as it is to incarcerate an American citizen. Immigration rules allow government officials to spot and locate such persons to make sure that they are never in a position to invoke those protections in the first place.

Deportation: "The Loss of Both Property and Life"

Deportation is the removal of an alien whose presence in the United States is no longer lawful. Common synonyms for "removal" include "elimination," "deletion," "subtraction," "amputation," and "deduction," all of which capture in various ways the process and feeling of deportation. Since the Act of 1990, the grounds for deportation have mirrored the grounds for exclusion: the government can deport persons who should never have been given permission to enter, or who never got permission in the first place; persons who commit "crimes of moral turpitude" or "aggravated felonies"; persons who have forged documents; persons who are terrorists or spies; and lastly, "any alien who, within five years after the date of entry, has become a public charge from causes not affirmatively shown to have arisen since entry."[18] Comparatively and historically, persons who had entered without inspection have made up the vast majority of deportees, with criminal aliens accounting for the second highest number. Between 1940 and 1980, only 407 aliens were deported because they had become a public charge, and even then, there were typically additional reasons to force their departure.[19]

Some grounds for deportation have raised serious issues involving core values in the United States constitution. For example, for over a hundred years, since the assassination of President William McKinley in 1901, federal statutes have provided for the deportation of "political undesirables." McKinley's assassin was either an anarchist, insane, or both, and although he was an American citizen, his ethnic name—Leon Czolgosz—was enough to trigger calls for the mass deportation of foreigners who were communists, subversives, and anarchists.[20] The federal courts, including the United States Supreme Court, upheld federal immigration rules like the ones passed in 1903, 1918, and 1920, all providing for the deportation of "anarchists," and this trend continued well into the 1950s.[21] After World War II, and in response to the establishment of the People's Republic of China in 1949, the Federal Bureau of Investigation worked closely with the Immigration Service to identify Asian American leftists likely to be sympathetic to the communist regime in mainland China. Although mass deportations of Chinese American leftists never materialized, historians tell us that, armed with the power to deport communists, "immigration authorities could easily intimidate Chinese American liberals and make their lives miserable."[22] Several prominent Supreme Court Justices—including Oliver Wendell Holmes and Hugo Black—spoke against these types of ideologically motivated deportations and exclusions, for they implicated free speech ideals in the First Amendment. Still, fewer than one thousand persons have been forcibly deported on ideological grounds since 1901.

Most deportations are not so dramatic. In fact, the vast majority of all deportable persons are not even forcibly removed. Since the Act of 1924, immigration rules have provided for "voluntary departure," meaning that aliens who are deportable have the chance to remove themselves without being forcibly removed. There were some benefits to this: if they admit "deportability" and leave, they may be allowed to return legally at some point in the future; if they do not, they may well be permanently barred from the United States. It is leniency for those who cooperate, harshness for those who resist. Many more people have chosen "voluntary departure" since the option became available: in 1961, about 8,000 people were deported and excluded, but over 52,000 people departed voluntarily. In 1991, about 33,000 persons were forcibly removed, while one million departed voluntarily.[23] The typical deportee who departs voluntarily entered the United States without inspection, violated no other law than the federal immigration law, and might very well try again to enter without inspection within a few days of his departure.

DEPORTATION ON CRIMINAL GROUNDS

The deportation of persons for having committed criminal offenses has always been popular in Congress as well as in the federal courts, and a criminal conviction has been the leading trigger for deportation proceedings. Since the landmark case *Fong Yue Ting v. United States,* a case in 1892 concerning the deportation of Chinese migrants apprehended in New York, the Supreme Court has upheld two basic principles: deportation can follow from unlawful acts, including unlawful presence in the United States; and deportation is not the same as "punishment" in the criminal law. Justice Holmes' prose during the Chinese Exclusion era is still helpful: in 1913, he wrote that deportation "is simply a refusal by the Government to harbor persons whom it does not want."[24] The idea was popular among government officials because civil proceedings were and are governed by a different set of rules, and persons facing deportation are still not afforded the more stringent legal protections enjoyed by those facing criminal charges. Someone facing deportation does not have the right against self-incrimination, for example, or the right to an attorney if one cannot afford one, or a right to a speedy "trial," or the right to a jury of one's peers. These are all concepts from the criminal law. Even today, "removal" remains a non-criminal matter—it is an issue to be settled between the United States (who typically wants to throw the person out) and the immigrant (who typically wants to remain), resolved through an odd set of modified civil procedures. The procedures appear odd because, despite the government's instance that this isn't punitive, it certainly does feel that way.[25]

Even the Supreme Court, which originally insisted that deportation was a non-punitive, non-criminal matter, has since acknowledged the gravity and severity of the stakes involved, and both the Court and Congress have provided for certain protections against abuses of government authority since the Exclusion era.[26] In one influential case involving a deportable Chinese alien, Justice Louis Brandeis said that "[deportation] may result also in loss of both property and life; or of all that makes life worth living."[27] In another influential case involving yet another deportable Chinese alien, Justice William Douglas agreed that deportation was indeed a very grave matter, such that when the lower federal courts disagreed about the terms under which an alien may be deported, the Supreme Court would tend toward compassion, because deportation was "the equivalent of banishment or exile."[28]

Because of decisions and sentiments like these, immigrants facing deportation have had a number of avenues to defend themselves from being thrown out, including the right to hire an attorney and the right to appeal adverse rulings several times (depending upon the grounds of removal), all the way up to the United States Supreme Court. But Justice Douglas's prose suggested that this could change: he and his colleagues "did not assume" that Congress would deport so easily. As we shall see, though, removal has become easier, more "streamlined," according to contemporary government officials, and many more persons are subject to removal for a wider array of offenses. Fewer avenues for appeal are now available. Rather than letting the federal courts assume anything, including a position based on mercy or compassion, Congress has spelled out quicker, easier, and broader avenues for persons to be deported in recent years. The changes were already apparent in the years leading up to the Act of 1990, in the first years of President Ronald Reagan's administration.

President Reagan had declared a "war on drugs" that entailed a new set of laws punishing a wide range of offenses within and beyond the boundaries of the United States. Now, the criminal sanctions attached to drug possession, use, and distribution account for an increasingly larger fraction of persons incarcerated for longer periods of time, both in state and in federal penitentiaries. The nexus between the drug war and deportation can be seen in rules like the Anti-Drug Abuse Act of 1988 (hereafter the Drug Act). The Drug Act defined an "aggravated felony" as a very serious crime, such as murder, kidnapping, weapons possession or distribution, often in tandem with drug trafficking. Aliens convicted of these "aggravated felonies" would be detained by federal authorities upon the completion of any criminal sentence, then they were to be deported. Special deportation proceedings—summary in nature, because of the lack of judicial review, and because various grounds of relief from deportation were denied—were created through the Act of 1988.

The Act of 1990 added several new rules for the deportation of criminal aliens very similar to the ones in the Act of 1988. Fifteen separate sections of the Act dealt with the deportation of any alien convicted of a crime of moral turpitude and of an aggravated felony. "Drug trafficking" and "any crime of violence ... for which the term of imprisonment imposed (regardless of any suspension of such imprisonment) is at least five years" were added to the definition of "aggravated felonies." The Attorney General was given additional authority to apprehend, detain, and deport criminal aliens—his officers were authorized to use firearms to arrest deportable aliens, and deportable criminal aliens had half the time (30 days, not 60) to request review of deportation orders by a federal judge. The Attorney General could issue a waiver for a final deportation order, but only if the deportable alien could show that his removal would cause "extreme hardship" to a child or spouse. All deportable criminal aliens aged fourteen and over were to be photographed and fingerprinted. Even if they left "voluntarily," all aliens deported on criminal grounds could not return to the United States for at least twenty years, whereas the previous bar had been ten years. Moreover, "an alien who has been convicted of an aggravated felony...may not apply for or be granted asylum."[29]

The reference to asylum is significant because asylum traditionally implied the government's willingness to protect a person from foreseeable harm—deportation provisions in the Act of 1990 were just the opposite of asylum. It was a complete turning away of the government from the person being removed. It reaffirmed the idea that although deportation was not a "punishment" in the strict technical sense, it was a form of banishment, which was the eviction of a subject from the protection of the sovereign, a penalty so severe that it was reserved in other legal systems only for those who were disloyal, treasonous, or incorrigible. It was the secular equivalent of excommunication.[30] By more aggressively deporting aliens convicted of crimes, the Act of 1990 was another step toward an immigration law designed to eliminate entirely the cost of these undesirables.

REFUGEE ADMISSIONS SINCE 1980 AND REFUGEE ADJUSTMENTS IN THE ACT OF 1990

For close to a quarter of a century now, the United States has accepted in a systemic way a special set of immigrants who have themselves been outcasts in or cast out of their own countries. Despite the fact that most of these persons typically arrive in the United States with virtually no property or wealth whatsoever, this special area of immigration law provides for the admissions of persons who are truly desperate. The Refugee Act of 1980 was a landmark piece of legislation that reframed principles in refugee and asylum policy found in older laws like the Displaced Persons Act of 1948 and the Refugee Relief Act of 1953. The Act of 1980 retained many of the features of these older rules, but clarified the exact terms for political asylum: anyone with a "well-founded fear of persecution" on the grounds of "race, nationality, religion, political opinion, or membership in a social group" can remain here or come here under the protection of the American government.[31] In theory, refugees are persons outside the United States who seek admission either because of past persecution or the likelihood of persecution. A person seeking asylum is someone who is already in the United States, but cannot or will not return because of a similar well founded fear of persecution. In both instances, their appeal to this country is based fundamentally on humanitarian grounds. To gain status as a refugee or asylee, such persons must not only show that their own governments consider them undesirables, but that they have very good reasons to fear harm should they return to their own country.[32]

Whether the United States accepts more than its fair share of refugees in the world has been a topic of considerable debate, but in the past two decades, influential legislators have moved to reframe refugee law so that *fewer* persons are admitted under this category.[33] Since 1980, refugees and asylees have constituted a significant fraction of the immigrant population, ranging anywhere from 6% to as high as 16% of all immigrants in a given year. Fiscal year 2001 was fairly typical: of the roughly 1 million persons admitted as immigrants or adjusting into immigrant status, refugees and asylees accounted for about 109,000 persons. However, according to the United Nations, there were in the late 1990s roughly 20 million "displaced persons" in the world, including 9 million just in Asia.[34] Influential lawmakers wondered whether the United States would suffer from "compassion fatigue" if it continued to admit large numbers of persons who had fled their countries, lost everything, and then relied on the United States financially and otherwise.[35]

Indeed, the Refugee Act of 1980 was passed in large part to ameliorate the refugee crises precipitated by American military involvement in Indochina. In the chaos following the civil wars in Vietnam, Cambodia, and Laos, several hundred thousand persons became displaced. By 1990, more than 120,000 persons from Cambodia, and more than 200,000 from Laos became permanent residents in the United States. By 2000, more than 700,000 persons from Vietnam settled as immigrants—mostly entering as refugees—in the United States. Only European refugees have settled here in greater numbers since World War II, and the vast majority of those were persons living within the now dissolved Soviet bloc.[36] In Asian American communities, first-generation Indochinese refugees and their immediate descendants now account for about 13% of the population of Asians in the United States, their influential presence a direct result of refugee admissions since the conclusion of the Vietnam War.[37]

However, there could have been even more refugee admissions had it not been for the Refugee Act of 1980. The rule was passed to *sort through* persons who were displaced for any number of reasons, including war and civil strife. By setting rather specific standards for persons seeking asylum, the Act of 1980 admitted only those who were "persecuted," not the larger universe of persons who were displaced but not necessarily persecuted. For example, if Vietnamese peasants were forced to move from their ancestral village because of American bombing, those facts alone would not be enough to gain asylum in the United States. Their displacement was certainly caused, in part, by American military involvement, but the Act of 1980 allows them to be admitted as refugees only if they can prove more—that they continue to have a legitimate fear of government authorities in communist Vietnam based on one of the five enumerated grounds in the Act of 1980. Because the grounds for asylum are thus limited, the Act of 1980 sifted displaced persons such that a sizable fraction of asylum and refugee claims have been subsequently denied, dismissed, or reviewed in greater detail. Since 1980, about 75% of asylum claims have been approved, the other quarter were denied, dismissed, or withdrawn. Since 1996, only about 60% of all asylum claims have been approved, but this was during a time when the population of displaced persons jumped by about five million persons.[38]

The reluctance to accept a wider range or greater number of displaced persons has no doubt hinged on the demographic and economic profile of refugee populations, particularly in recent decades. Refugees in general tend to be very poor; fleeing persecution, literally running for their lives, a great many refugees lost everything, have nothing, arrive with nothing, and so depend upon the states that have admitted them as refugees. They are precisely the type of people most likely to become a public charge. Indeed, according to Bill Ong Hing, a scholar of Asian immigration, "Nationwide, 64 percent of all Southeast Asian households headed by refugees arriving after 1980 are on public assistance, three times the rate of African Americans and four times that of Latinos." This assessment was based on figures collected in the late 1980s. According to figures from the last census, much had remained the same: about 40 percent of children of Vietnamese immigrants in New York were in households below the federal poverty line, over a third of their peers in Los Angeles and Orange Counties were in the same position.[39] If anything, the economic conditions for Laotian and Cambodian immigrants were even worse.[40] A majority of these families were classified as "welfare-dependent." Many Laotian and Cambodian refugees were illiterate in their native countries; some had never lived in a cash economy, nor dealt in any meaningful way with government bureaucracies. Other refugees—mostly from Central American and the Caribbean Island nations, especially Cuba and Haiti—were equally impoverished.

The settlement of Southeast Asian refugees was such a massive and coordinated effort that it represented a special case in contemporary American immigration law. Because of the formal military involvement of the United States in Southeast Asia, the United States government had established special guidelines for the settlement of Southeast Asian refugees since 1976. To lessen the economic impact of refugee settlements on local communities, for example, President Jimmy Carter's administration had attempted to disperse Indochinese refugees throughout the United States, as though this dispersal would both help local communities cope with any increased demands for services and hasten the need for the refugees themselves to assimilate into American life. This policy mostly did not work.[41] Indochinese refugees resettled in distinct communities—for instance, the Laotians and the ethnic Hmong from Laos remigrated to places like Richmond, California, and to the California Central Valley, as well as into the Minneapolis-St. Paul region. Vietnamese resettled along the Gulf Coast, often as fishermen in Texas and Louisiana, and they also moved to northern Virginia, Boston, San Jose, and most visibly, Orange County, California. One of the largest concentrations of Cambodians outside of Cambodia is now in Long Beach, south of Los Angeles, although sizable numbers live as far apart as Lowell, Massachusetts, and San Francisco. This resettlement of Southeast Asian refugees within distinct regions of the United States—coupled with their relatively high rates of poverty—made them both very visible and often resented. Local authorities phrased many of these communities as large-scale social problems directly tied to an over-generous, misguided immigration policy.

Overall, the relatively high numbers of refugees settling in the United States by 1990 caused many legislators to worry whether this form of admission was becoming a kind of back door for poorer immigrants around the world. Again, Senator Alan Simpson of Wyoming, as the chair of the Immigration Subcommittee, proposed several rules that attempted to limit the numbers of persons claiming refugee status or asylum in the United States after the Act of 1980.[42] He was incredulous when Chinese asylum seekers, for example, wanted to claim refugee status to avoid China's one-child policy, and he was equally incredulous when certain Central Americans refused to return to their home countries for fear of their lives. Simpson and several other influential legislators claimed that a significant fraction of such refugee and asylee claims were actually exaggerated—the true motive lay in a desire to flee deplorable economic conditions, not persecution.[43] In 1994, in a debate about yet another refugee amendment, this one providing for the admission of Eastern European and Russian refugees, Simpson said: "It appears to me that our refugee program has become for the most part an immigration program in refugee clothing, and with refugee funding."[44]

During that same year, in her public testimony, the Chairperson of the President's Commission on Legal Immigration Reform, former Congresswoman Barbara Jordan—who had been one of the greatest champions of civil rights legislation in Congress—said that while the United States should continue to admit refugees at about 50,000 persons per year, subsequent legislation was needed to clarify the criteria under which refugees were selected, so as to avoid "abuses" in the system of political asylum. The

Commission also reported that, in general, it was exploring whether immigration rules should be reoriented to limit the numbers of persons who might become dependent upon public assistance.[45]

Finally, in the November elections of 1994, Republicans became a majority in Congress after four decades of Democratic control. Republican leaders had promised a new "Contract With America," provisions of which included new rules designed to underscore "Personal Responsibility," "The Taking Back of Our Streets," and "Family Reinforcement." Several proposed rules in the Contract called for eliminating or severely curtailing public assistance for non-citizens, which were in spirit much like the provisions of Proposition 187 in California, the statewide ballot measure that had passed by a two-thirds margin in the November elections of 1994.[46]

By the end of 1994, when the Contract With America was selling briskly across the country, a wide segment of the American public seemed to be expressing some kind of "compassion fatigue," including a general aversion to poorer legal and illegal immigrants, as well as an overall skepticism about whether laws like the Refugee Act of 1980 were appropriately sifting through those seeking asylum in the United States from those just seeking the United States. The closing off of asylum to criminal aliens in the Act of 1990 and the public remarks about asylum abuse, immigrants, and welfare in 1994 were each harbingers of much harsher changes to the immigration law in 1996. Indeed, the new rules would impose considerable barriers against persons who had always been regarded as excludable or unwanted, but to the point of eliminating or excising such persons with greater facility than ever before.

PART II
The Unwanted

CHAPTER 4

Efficiency and Cost: Detention and Deportation under the Acts of 1996

Driven in large part by the "political revolution" in 1994 that swept Republicans into Congress and gave ardent opponents of illegal immigration a tremendous victory in California, both Congress and the Clinton Administration proposed another set of laws to limit the migration of the poor and unskilled into the United States. Also, by providing for summary deportation and removal proceedings, immigration law gave public officials new methods to cut out more quickly and efficiently persons who violated the criminal law. All of these contemporary rules had analogs in the past, but substantively, the immigration rules passed in 1996 were part of a much larger move in the law to become harsher and tougher on "persons likely to be a public charge." Instead of a war on poverty, Congress did seem to be stepping up a "war against the poor."[1] Rhetorically, the changes in policy were about increasing "efficiency," "personal responsibility," and "enhancing public safety," which meant being tougher on crime and forcing the poor to be less dependent upon public assistance. After all, "changing welfare as we know it" was a campaign promise made by Presidential candidate Bill Clinton in 1992, and by 1994, Republicans in Congress were eager to take up this offer with renewed fervor.

These changes in the political climate would have race-based consequences, as we will argue. Although Central American and Mexican immigrants would bear the full brunt of these rules, poorer Asian immigrants and families would also be profoundly affected. In fact, these laws have shaped and are reshaping Asian American communities, though in many respects, they will no doubt tend to give the impression that Asians in the United States are a unique racial group, more likely to be professionals in suburbs rather than poorer persons in inner cities. This is because poorer persons, including poorer Asians, would be much less likely to be admitted in the first place, and many more of them would become subject to deportation under the rules eventually passed in 1996.

CRIMINAL DETENTION AND DEPORTATION: "NOT SUBJECT TO REVIEW BY ANY COURT."

As much as "compassion fatigue," several years before the events of September 11, 2001, immigration rules were also increasingly driven by a politics of fear. In March of 1993, one month after a car bomb exploded in the parking garage beneath the World Trade Center, Congress heard testimony calling for tighter immigration controls to combat organized terrorist groups. By that time, the suspects in the World Trade Center attack were reported to have ties to terrorist groups in the Middle East and northern Africa. Similar testimony over the next several months from public officials and from experts in arms control and international relations convinced many members of Congress that terrorist activities and immigration issues were intimately related. The relative ease with which tourists and other non-immigrants could enter the country left wide open the possibility that those who wished to harm Americans could do so without worrying about immigration enforcement. Many of the warnings were ominous, and suggested threats to the very core of American values: "In the worse case, the federal government is in danger of failing to meet its constitutional responsibilities to 'provide for the common defense' and to 'secure the blessings of liberty to ourselves and our posterity.'" These threats included "nuclear attacks," especially the smuggling of nuclear materials for radioactive "dirty bombs" detonated near the centers of major American cities.[2]

The bombing of the Alfred Murrah federal building in Oklahoma City in April 1995 accelerated political efforts to pass an anti-terrorism bill in Congress—one with significant immigration provisions—for the remainder of the year, even though the suspects apprehended for the attack in Oklahoma City were not foreigners. Before the formal charges were filed against Timothy McVeigh and his accomplices, many had speculated that this was another act of terrorism perpetrated by groups based abroad.[3] The Anti-Terrorism and Effective Death Penalty Act, or "AEDPA" (hereafter the Anti-Terrorism Act), was passed one year after the Oklahoma City bombing, in April of 1996.

The primary portions of the Anti-Terrorism Act were designed to deter terrorism, to provide justice for its victims, and to prevent the entry of, as well as for removal of, persons dangerous to American national security. But the Anti-Terrorism Act gave the Attorney General broad authority in matters related to immigration enforcement. For example, the Attorney General could exclude persons with probable connections to international terrorists, and this exclusion would preclude any judicial review.[4] In addition, a broader range of persons—whether involved in terrorism or not—could be deported for a much wider range of offenses. The Act of 1990 had provided for the deportation of aliens committing criminal offenses: any alien becomes deportable if he commits a crime of moral turpitude within five years after the date of entry, and "either is sentenced to confinement or is confined therefor in a prison or correctional institution for one year or longer." The Anti-Terrorism Act replaced this language: any alien who commits a crime of moral turpitude within five years after the date of entry and "is convicted of a crime for which a sentence of one year or longer *may* be imposed."[5]

This was a crucial distinction—now, any alien *who could have been sentenced* to a year or longer for a criminal offense was deportable. Moreover, "any final order of deportation against an alien who is deportable by reason of having committed a criminal offense ... shall not be subject to review by any court."[6] Deportation procedures were made more summary in this way, with far fewer orders of deportation eligible for either administrative relief from the Attorney General (who could grant waivers of final deportation orders) or for judicial review. The law also required that those who posed any kind of risk to public safety ought to be detained prior to deportation. Although immigration detention would end upon deportation, Congress did not specify how long this detention could last in theory—indeed, in subsequent challenges to the Anti-Terrorism Act, its defenders suggested that immigration detention for criminal aliens could be *indefinite* even in instances where deportation was not likely in the foreseeable future.[7]

Since the Immigration Reform and Control Act of 1986, federal policy makers had attempted to streamline criminal deportation, which would involve a coordinated effort between local, state, and federal authorities. Federal power to affect deportation would also be distributed more widely: state and local law enforcement agencies were authorized to detain non-citizens just for immigration enforcement purposes.[8] The Act also authorized the Immigration Service to create a national database to identify non-citizens convicted of crimes, which would be shared with local and state law enforcement agencies for deportation purposes.[9] Several Congressional leaders chastised the Immigration Service for failing to fully implement the Institutional Hearing Program (IHP), which until then was a relatively unknown and under-funded program created through the Act of 1986. Under this program, federal authorities were to work closely with state prison officials to identify and deport criminal aliens upon their release from state prisons; several prominent politicians, including Lamar Smith of Texas, criticized the Immigration Service for failing to use this program more effectively to deport criminal aliens from the United States before 1996. In testimony leading to and following the Anti-Terrorism Act, officials in the Clinton Administration promised to step up efforts to facilitate more deportations in response to intense Congressional oversight of programs like the IHP.[10]

In commenting on these trends, one leading scholar of deportation, Daniel Kanstroom, noted that rules like the Anti-Terrorism Act were part of what has evolved into "a rather complete convergence between the criminal justice and deportation systems."[11] The debate over deportation as a form of punishment itself has its roots in the Chinese Exclusion period, as was discussed in Chapter 2. Clearly, persons with criminal convictions were always subject to exclusion as well as deportation. And although American judges had long debated whether deportation was an *additional* punishment after a criminal conviction, every alien with a criminal conviction has always been subject to deportation. But even in light of such a conviction, deportable aliens in the past could seek relief if their deportation would cause "serious economic detriment to a citizen or legally resident alien who [was] the spouse, parent, or minor child of such deportable alien."[12] Rules like the Anti-Terrorism Act forbade these forms of relief, as though systemically denying mercy to all aliens convicted of crimes.

Previous rules attempted to adjust immigration consequences for criminal convictions by considering the impact of deportation on the deportee and his intimates. Since 1952, relief from deportation could be available to an alien showing "exceptional and extremely unusual hardship to himself or to his spouse, parent, or child," a standard that has been litigated repeatedly ever since 1952. In most cases, factors considered under this standard included medical conditions, the age of minor children affected by the alien's removal, and the cumulative difficulties of adjusting to life in the place where the alien's deportation was imminent.[13]

The principle of relief had deeper roots, as some courts "pardoned" aliens who had served criminal sentences so that they would not be subsequently deported. We can see an example of this practice in the decision of a Circuit Court in a case from 1926, involving the deportation of an alien to Poland following his criminal conviction. The petitioner Klonis had not been pardoned, but the Court extended him another opportunity to receive a pardon for these reasons:

> Whether the relator came here in arms or at the age of ten, he is as much our product as though his mother had borne him on American soil. He knows no other language, no other people, no other habits, than ours; he will be as much a stranger in Poland as any one born of ancestors who immigrated in the seventeenth century. However heinous his crimes, deportation is to him exile, a dreadful punishment, abandoned by the common consent of all civilized peoples. Such, indeed, it would be to any one, but to one already proved to be incapable of honest living, a helpless waif in a strange land, it will be utter destruction. That our reasonable efforts to rid ourselves of unassimilable immigrants should in execution be attended by such a cruel and barbarous result would be a national reproach.[14]

We reprinted the Court's reasoning here because it speaks to a set of similar cases that have arisen since the passage of the new deportation rules in 1996. If, as the Circuit Court found, it was cruel and barbarous for the nation to expel a "helpless waif in a strange land," was it still cruel and barbarous to expel similarly situated persons to places like Cambodia? The law was becoming stripped of such moral reservations.

In fact, after 1996, courts were forbidden from considering these humanitarian issues as they pertained to the immigrant facing deportation: "there was little doubt [that] Congress intended to make it more difficult for aliens to obtain relief."[15] Instead of relief, a more common trajectory was toward an efficient transfer, from the end of a criminal sentence in a state prison to the beginning of deportation proceedings in a federal detention facility. Even for those who "know no other language, no other people, no other habits, than ours," the fact of their non-citizen status could far outweigh any countervailing equities, or long-standing practices of mercy or relief.

For legislators like Lamar Smith, though, the justification for this change in policy hinged upon a primary concern for the safety of American citizens and for their tax money: "These criminal aliens are a drain of the American taxpayer while they are in prison ... and when they get out, they pose a significant threat to the public safety."[16] By 1996, this language of efficiency and public safety clearly superseded concerns about the impact of deportation on the immigrant deportee or his family.

A few months after the Anti-Terrorism Act, Congress also passed the Illegal Immigration Reform and Immigrant Responsibility Act of 1996, or "IIRIRA" (hereafter the Responsibility Act), another rule that carried forth similar themes. For example, one of the most important changes to immigration law under the Responsibility Act was embodied in a new concept that combined exclusion and deportation proceedings into a common set of procedures for "removal." "Excludable" aliens were now "inadmissible" aliens, who, because they were already illegally in the United States, were not "admitted" in a strictly legal sense.[17] "Deportable" aliens were still "deportable," but their deportability would be determined in the context of new "removal proceedings," and relief from deportation was rephrased as "cancellation of removal."

Under the new scheme, anyone who did not make a legal "admission into the United States," or anyone who was deportable subsequent to admission, thus had their cases adjudicated through the same set of legal procedures. The procedures suggested that Congress had greatly anticipated widescale illegal or fraudulent entry into the United States. For presumptively "inadmissible aliens," removal proceedings were to be "expedited," meaning that aliens in such circumstances had only one motion to reconsider an adverse finding. Several critics charged that this summary process would be excessively harsh against those seeking asylum: one said that the Responsibility Act "[wiped out asylum] as we know it, replacing it with a much stricter process."

First, if the Attorney General determines that a person applying for asylum can be safely moved to a third country, that person may not apply for asylum. Second, all petitions for asylum must be filed within one year of entering the United States. According to leading scholars of refugee law, "Despite the fact that most genuine refugees were not able to apply within one year of their arrival, members of the 104th Congress were intent on imposing a deadline, apparently under the belief that such a bar was necessary to prevent time-consuming adjudication of fraudulent applications."[18] The process itself gave broad discretion to relatively low-level immigration officials at the nation's borders. Most importantly, "a decision by the Attorney General to bar an alien from applying for asylum [was] not subject to judicial review." In all instances, persons at the border could be detained pending final removal orders, and certain "inadmissible aliens"—namely those convicted of crimes—were completely barred from judicial review of final removal orders under the Responsibility Act.[19]

As in the Anti-Terrorism Act, the Responsibility Act also expanded definitions of aggravated felonies that could become the grounds for deportation. Critics of the rule noted that the threshold for deportation on criminal grounds had become so low that relatively minor crimes—a forged check, public urination, or shoplifting—could trigger deportation. Indeed, this proved to be true: since 1996, deportation proceedings have been initiated against aliens convicted of, among other things, drunk-driving offenses, domestic-violence offenses, child abuse and child neglect, and drug possession.[20] Moreover, when these rules were initially passed, government officials moved to apply them retroactively—literally, any aliens who had been convicted of an aggravated felony were subject to deportation, irrespective of when that conviction occurred, and their removal could be accomplished through "expedited proceedings."[21] Overall, in the words of one law professor, "the new immigration laws increase the likelihood that a permanent resident will face mandatory deportation for any criminal conviction."[22]

The Responsibility Act was a major shift in the law of deportation, not just because it eliminated forms of relief that had been afforded to those facing deportation even on criminal grounds. More importantly, for all non-citizens, the rules mandating detention and removal were like a stern warning designed to heighten a sense of anxiety before the law. All non-citizens—no matter the length of their residence in the United States, or the intensity of their attachments to their families and neighborhoods, or their ability to reenter society after a criminal sentence—could be deported for a single criminal conviction. A single drunk-driving conviction, a single conviction for child abuse, a conviction for shoplifting—whether these were infractions that could occur in the future, or were part of an immigrant's record in the past—all could become the grounds for a permanent exile from the United States. The Responsibility Act seemed to authorize what is now called "retroactive deportations": based on a past criminal conviction, a non-citizen could be placed in removal proceedings even though his conviction and sentence had occurred long before the enactment of the Responsibility Act in 1996.[23] Any non-citizen who had had a criminal conviction could legitimately expect federal authorities to find him and place him in removal proceedings; any non-citizen charged with a crime should now be worried less about the criminal sentence, and much more about the "collateral consequences" of that criminal sentence, namely deportation. Indeed, for criminal defense attorneys who handle immigrant clients, removal has become a much more pressing concern that shapes their defense strategies and bargaining positions in criminal proceedings. In the majority of cases, the actual criminal charge or sentence would be far less draconian than the prospect of permanent removal.[24]

The Responsibility Act was even harsher to yet another class of prospective wrongdoers, these being illegal immigrants along the southern border. In fact, the vast majority of the Responsibility Act concerned methods to deter illegal entry into the United States.[25] They are only briefly summarized here, although the scholarly literature on the new exclusionary measures has grown voluminous since 1996.[26] In general, the Responsibility Act provided millions of dollars for new Border Patrol agents, high-technology surveillance equipment, electric fences, lights, and other barriers to deter illegal crossings along the southern border. The Act accelerated a process scholars have called the "militarization of the border," a policy of converting what was a legal and fictive barrier into an actual, physical one, replete with steel, concrete, and fencing.[27] All of these were organized under Title I of the Responsibility Act, and all of these measures had had the early support of key public officials in the Clinton Administration, including Attorney General Janet Reno and Doris Meissner, the Commissioner of the Immigration and Naturalization Service. In their testimony to Congress, they accepted the idea of using these new and powerful measures to deter illegal entry.[28]

Many of the obstacles would quickly prove lethal. These technologies and border patrols were designed to deter illegal immigrants near popular urban centers where such persons had crossed in large numbers before, places near San Diego, Nogales, El Paso, and Brownsville. New man-made barriers in those areas were intended to take advantage of the fact that the surrounding less populated regions were so dangerous and remote that most persons would not attempt such crossings in the freezing mountains or in the withering deserts. But between 1998 and 2002, about three hundred to four hundred persons have died crossing these treacherous areas every year. Most died of exposure or dehydration. According to Wayne Cornelius, a leading scholar of immigration policy, by 2003, "the killing grounds—the mountains of east San Diego County, the deserts and irrigation canals of California and Arizona, the railroad yards and truck stops of Texas—have yielded 2,355 victims since 1995, and the bodies of hundreds of others undoubtedly await discovery."[29] Because so many undocumented aliens have died along the southern border, and because the United States government knew that this was a likely result of the enhanced measures authorized in laws like the Responsibility Act of 1996, Cornelius and others have described these policies as "immoral."

But to stress their immorality, however, may be to stress the wrong thing. "Immorality" comes from a language of ethics; the new immigration rules governing removal and exclusion could more aptly be described as "amoral," to the extent that much of their justification came from the language of the market, from an analysis based on a mandate to reduce costs and increase efficiencies in immigration policy. For example, in his report to Congress in September of 1996, David Martin, the General Counsel for the INS, repeatedly used phrases referring to the "strategic use of detention capacities," the development of a "comprehensive tracking method," and greater efforts to "[analyze] the most efficient steps that can be taken to hasten our progress toward maximum removals of criminal aliens."[30]

Similarly, officials from the Executive Office for Immigration Review reported that roughly 180 immigration judges throughout the United States were attempting to clear over 218,000 immigration cases per year, sometimes by using such innovative technologies as teleconferencing immigration hearings, or by holding hearings in "Port Court," a kind of one-stop immigration hearing in an airport or some other port of entry. Teleconferencing an immigration hearing meant that the immigration judge and the immigrant would only experience one another through a television monitor. Port Court meant that immigrants would appear at the airport, for instance, have their immigration issues settled in "Port Court," then "immediately be released from detention and deported to their country of nationality." "This avoids additional detention costs that would otherwise be borne by U.S. taxpayers."[31] In the following month, Doris Meissner insisted that this type of stretching of government resources marked "an era of progress and achievement."[32] It was, in a sense, the systemic development of an efficient system of removal and exclusion that privileged taxpayers' money over conventional and more expensive notions of due process, or even mercy.

LITIGATING DETENTION AND DEPORTATION

In two important cases, the federal courts tempered the impact of the Anti-Terrorism Act and the Responsibility Act on non-citizens facing removal on criminal grounds. In *INS v. St. Cyr*, a case that had moved up to the Supreme Court by 2001, portions of both laws were determined to be against established precedents. In that case, the alien from Haiti, Enrico St. Cyr, was deportable because of a state conviction for selling a controlled substance, a classic trigger for deportation on criminal grounds. He was charged with possession of and intent to distribute about $75 worth of cocaine, although authorities had suspected that he was probably a major narcotics trafficker. Prior to both rules, though, he was eligible for a waiver of deportation during his removal proceedings, granted at the discretion of the Attorney General; in response to St. Cyr's petition for a waiver, the Attorney General insisted that he was no longer within his discretion to grant one, despite the fact that St. Cyr's conviction occurred *before* the passage of the new rules. St. Cyr thus faced a variant of "retroactive deportation."

A narrow majority agreed with the immigrant plaintiff, saying that he should be eligible for a waiver, in part because he had made his plea agreement in Connecticut for the drug conviction without accounting for (and not being able to account for) the immigration consequences detailed in the Acts of 1996. Had he known that the Attorney General no longer had discretion to waive final deportation orders, or had he known that all federal courts were precluded from reviewing his case prior to his deportation, all of the parties in his case might have weighed the options more carefully. "The potential for unfairness in retroactive application of the [Responsibility Act] to people like ... St. Cyr is significant and manifest."[33] Justice Stevens continued:

> Relying upon settled practice, the advice of counsel, and perhaps even assurances in open court that the entry of the plea would not foreclose ... relief, a great number of defendants in ... St. Cyr's position agreed to plead guilty. Now that prosecutors have received the benefit of these plea agreements, agreements that were likely facilitated by the aliens' belief in their continued eligibility for ... relief, it would surely be contrary to 'familiar considerations of fair notice, reasonable reliance, and settled expectations,' to hold that [the Responsibility Act's] subsequent restrictions deprive them of any possibility of such relief.[34]

In other words, because removal was not a "settled expectation" facing St. Cyr in his Connecticut criminal case, and because he had no reason to think that he would be ineligible for relief, it would be unfair to deny him access to that form of relief. Antonin Scalia, Sandra Day O'Connor, William Rehnquist, and Clarence Thomas complained in a sharply worded dissent that the majority was contradicting the will of Congress, which was clearly to expedite the removal of persons like St. Cyr, and precisely by denying them either judicial review or discretionary waivers.[35]

In another set of cases, also decided by the Supreme Court in 2001, portions of the Anti-Terrorism and Responsibility Acts were ruled unconstitutional as they pertained to the practice of "indefinite detention." Two petitioners—Kestutis Zadvydas and Kim Ho Ma—were being held indefinitely by the INS because they were both "undeportable." Zadvydas was "a resident alien who was born, apparently of Lithuanian parents, in a displaced persons camp in Germany in 1948. When he was eight years old,

Zadvydas immigrated to the United States with his parents and other family members, and he has lived here ever since."[36] Since early adulthood, Zadvydas had had trouble with the law, and he was now facing deportation. But neither Germany nor Lithuania would take him, as neither country recognized him as a citizen.

His fellow petitioner, Kim Ho Ma, was born in Cambodia in 1977. When he was two, his family fled, taking him to refugee camps in Thailand and the Philippines and eventually to the United States, where he has lived as a resident alien since the age of eleven." He, too, was subsequently convicted of a serious crime: In 1995, at age 17, Ma was involved in a gang-related shooting, convicted of manslaughter, and sentenced to 38 months' imprisonment. He served two years, after which he was released into INS custody. That was in 1999; for the next two years, the INS unsuccessfully attempted to remove Ma to Cambodia, which also refused to accept him. Could, then, the INS detain deportable criminal aliens like Zadvydas or Ma when there was no "realistic chance" that they would ever be removed? By 1999, when Ma's case first appeared in the Ninth Circuit Court of Appeals, over one hundred deportable criminal aliens were in similar circumstances, and federal judges deciding these cases—many involving Southeast Asian immigrants—had produced contradictory approaches to the law.[37] Zadvydas lost his indefinite detention case in the Fifth Circuit Court of Appeals, whereas Ma had prevailed in his own argument against the INS in the Ninth Circuit.

The Supreme Court's Justices in *Zadvydas v. Davis* were as divided as the lower federal courts. Speaking for a narrow 5–4 majority, Justice Breyer held that "[any] statute permitting indefinite detention of an alien would raise a serious constitutional problem" under the Due Process Clause of the Fifth Amendment. It was an even greater problem because detention in the context of removal proceedings was civil in nature: "The civil confinement here at issue is not limited, but potentially permanent." Under current procedures established by the INS, the INS had ninety days to remove an alien. After that, if a detainee was still in custody, and that person was facing indefinite detention, then he had to prove affirmatively that he was not a danger to the community. This "hearing" was an administrative process not necessarily subject to judicial review. Breyer noted that "the Constitution demands greater procedural protection even for property."[38]

Yet in his central holding, Breyer did not order the release of either Zadvydas or Ma, but rather did suggest a more rigorous level of "procedural protections" to determine whether they could be held further.[39] At best, the ruling in *Zadvydas* was a partial victory, and as recently as 2003, the Supreme Court approved the use of detention to effect removal on criminal grounds, even in cases where the Immigration Service did not determine whether a deportable alien posed a threat to the community.[40]

In his dissenting opinion in *Zadvydas*, Justice Anthony Kennedy listed a number of cases where "dangerous individuals" might be subsequently released "in our community," as if to underscore the danger to public safety that could result from the majority opinion. Most of the cases involved Southeast Asian immigrants: "[Saroeut] Ourk was convicted of rape by use of drugs in conjunction with the kidnapping of a 13-year-old girl; after serving 18 months of his prison term, he was released on parole but was returned to custody twice more for parole violations …. When he was ordered deported and transferred to the custody of the INS, it is no surprise the INS determined he was both a flight risk and a danger to the community." Justice Kennedy mentioned other deportable criminal aliens from Southeast Asia—men with names like "Phetsany," "Mounsaveng," "Lim," and "Phuong": "Today's result will ensure these dangerous individuals, and hundreds more like them, will remain free while the Executive Branch tries to secure their removal."[41] Southeast Asians were central to this issue and were particularly problematic, as their "native" countries refused to admit persons deported from the United States. This meant that by 2001, about one third of the INS' indefinite detainees were of Southeast Asian ancestry.

THE PACE AND IMPACT OF MASS REMOVAL

Justice Kennedy's concerns about deportable Southeast Asians were addressed by executive officials under President George Bush, and far more quickly than many had expected. On March 22, 2002, the United States and the Royal Government of Cambodia signed a repatriation agreement, providing in part that "all costs of repatriation, including air transportation and escort service, should be borne exclusively by the requesting state." Although the two parties said that this agreement was part of a much larger process to "further enhance cooperative and friendly relations between the two states," several Cambodian officials insisted that their nation was forced into the agreement by the United States, which threatened to withhold foreign aid to Cambodia if it did not sign.[42] National advocacy groups representing Southeast Asian immigrants protested the agreement as well, because the removal of Cambodians would entail "the forcible deportation of people to [a] country they fled as refugees."[43]

The sudden possibility of removal of persons to Cambodia did raise several serious issues. Many of the Cambodian immigrants living in the

United States had left their native country over three decades of political turmoil. Following the withdrawal of American troops from Indochina in 1975, the proto-communist Khmer Rouge took control of Cambodia by forcing the departure of the Cambodian king; the leaders of the Khmer Rouge, including Pol Pot, abolished money and private property, identified, tortured, and assassinated former government officials and virtually anyone who had had meaningful contact with either the French or the Americans, and then emptied the cities of Cambodia, including Phnom Penh, to force all urban dwellers to work in agricultural collectives in rural areas. As many as one million Cambodians may have lost their lives from 1975 to 1978, mostly due to starvation. In 1978, Vietnamese forces would enter and occupy Cambodia for the next ten years, and they initially forced the departure of the Khmer Rouge. Although Vietnamese forces occupied Cambodia, they could not prevent guerilla warfare in more remote areas of Cambodia, and this warfare in turn generated thousands of political and economic refugees. Thousands of Cambodians also lost their lives during this period.[44]

Most of the roughly 72,000 Cambodians who came to the United States were admitted as refugees *after* Pol Pot had been deposed. In fact, American executive officials began ordering the admission of Cambodians as refugees to protest the Vietnamese invasion of Cambodia.[45] In 1991, a peace agreement eventually resulted in the establishment of a constitutional monarchy in Cambodia. But by 2000, the population of persons of Cambodian ancestry in the United States—many of whom were minors dependent upon their parents who had gained refugee status—numbered about 171,000. By the time that the United States and the Royal Government of Cambodia had "agreed" to the repatriation of Cambodian nationals deported from the United States, about 1,500 Cambodian immigrants were facing removal. About 4,500 Vietnamese immigrants and 2,000 Laotian immigrants were in similar circumstances. Within a year of the Cambodian repatriation agreement, about forty persons had been deported to Cambodia. By the end of 2003, about seventy had been removed. Of the Cambodians facing removal, their average age upon arrival in the United States was nine years old, they spoke little or no Khmer, and they had been in the United States an average of twenty years.[46] In many respects, they resembled the protagonist in *Klonis,* the "helpless waif" for whom deportation would have "[been] utter destruction." Whereas the federal court had saved Klonis from "such a cruel and barbarous" removal, recent Southeast Asian immigrants have not been shown the same mercy.

In April of 2001, Representative Barney Frank, a Democrat from Massachusetts, proposed a bill that would allow cancellation of removal for persons ordered removed based on a criminal conviction for a "non-violent" aggravated felony. For non-citizens who had committed a violent felony, cancellation would be available if they had been admitted into the United States before the age of 16. The proposed Family Reunification Act would also allow some persons who had been removed to return to the United States and seek adjustment as permanent residents. The bill collected only one Republican co-sponsor, and it has yet to pass into law because of stiff Republican opposition throughout Congress. After the events of September 11th, most commentators, including Representative Frank himself, doubted that this bill would ever pass.[47]

The story of Cambodian immigrants facing criminal deportation was a relatively small part of the much larger, faster pace of deportation in the United States since 1996. In 1986, fewer than 3,000 persons were removed on the grounds of a criminal conviction; in 1996, about 38,000 persons were removed; that figure increased to 55,000 persons in 1998; and by 2000, it was over 70,000 persons.[48] Table 4.1 shows removal statistics for 2001: of the roughly 170,000 formally removed by the Immigration Service, more than 71,000 persons were removed on criminal grounds. A significantly smaller fraction of Asian immigrants were removed overall, but some Asian groups—immigrants from the Philippines or from South Korea—were more likely than average to be removed on criminal grounds. All Southeast Asians facing removal had been placed in such proceedings because of a prior criminal conviction.

But in fiscal year 2001, all Asian immigrants constituted less than 2 percent of all removals. Mexican, Central American, and South American immigrants have obviously borne the brunt of these new policies, and far more severely than any other immigrant group. Based on government projections, this is a trend that is not likely to change in the near future.

Table 4.2 lists the types of criminal convictions that were the leading grounds for removal in fiscal year 2001. Drug convictions remained the most common reason for removal, making up 41% of all removals based on a criminal conviction. The origins of the deportation and removal provisions of the Acts of 1990 and 1996 were rooted in the Anti-Drug Abuse Act of 1988, an enduring legacy of President Reagan's "war on drugs," so it might be fitting that drug convictions were the central driving force behind immigrant removals. Again, preliminary reports from the Immigration Service suggest that drug convictions will remain the leading grounds for removal from the United States.[49]

Scholars are just beginning to measure and assess the impact of mass detention and mass removal on immigrant communities in the United States, especially after the Patriot Act of 2001.[50] Such mass removal has had

TABLE 4.1 Formal Removals in 2001

	Number removed	Percent	Number of criminals	Percent of criminals in number removed
All	176,984	100.00%	71,597	40.45%
Top 9 Nations				
Mexico	141,133	79.74%	57,144	40.49%
Honduras	4,338	2.45%	1,314	30.29%
Guatemala	4,235	2.39%	1,094	25.83%
Dominican Republic	3,935	2.22%	2,135	54.26%
El Salvador	3,722	2.10%	1,812	48.68%
Colombia	2,182	1.23%	1,455	66.68%
Jamaica	2,008	1.13%	1,292	64.34%
Brazil	1,645	0.93%	79	4.80%
Canada	1,097	0.62%	633	57.70%
All Asia	3,158	1.78%	1,003	31.76%
PRC	492	0.28%	114	23.17%
Philippines	457	0.26%	284	62.14%
India	375	0.21%	71	18.93%
Pakistan	332	0.19%	57	17.17%
Korea	263	0.15%	109	41.44%
Indonesia	222	0.13%	14	6.31%

Source: Immigration and Naturalization Service Statistical Yearbook 236, 254 (2001).

tremendous impacts on several levels—for the persons removed, for their families, for the broader communities in which they lived, and for the places to which they have been removed. For example, no one knows how Cambodian deportees will adjust to life in a place where they truly are strangers—most have absolutely no memory of a "life" in Cambodia, and with a criminal record from the United States and very little support of any kind, it would be difficult to imagine how these persons will ever adjust successfully. Cambodian officials and American observers in Cambodia speculated that many of these persons would eventually resort again to some form of criminal activity in order to survive.[51] If about seventy Cambodian deportees could raise such severe concerns in Cambodia, it is

TABLE 4.2 Formal Removals Based on Criminal Grounds in 2001

Crime	Number removed	Percent of total crime
Dangerous drugs	29,356	41
Immigration	12,585	18
Assault	6,580	9
Burglary	2,671	4
Robbery	2,640	4
Larceny	1,787	2
Sexual assaults	1,741	2
Family offences	1,422	2
Traffic offenses	1,344	2
Forgery	1,220	2

Source: Immigration and Naturalization Service Statistical Yearbook 236 (2001).

even more difficult to imagine how Mexican law and society could cope with about 60,000 criminal deportees from the United States *every year.*

Moreover, the ease with which persons can now be removed can have devastating effects on immigrant families. Scholars have long worried that immigrant women, for example, were relatively unprotected in the law with respect to domestic violence.[52] In response to these concerns, Congress enacted the Violence Against Women Act in 1994 to provide immigrant women with protection against adverse immigration consequences when they reported spousal abuse.[53] Since 1996, however, a single conviction for domestic abuse easily qualifies as a criminal ground for removal—advocates have since wondered whether such a harsh result might *deter* immigrant women from reporting instances of domestic violence, fearing that their spouses might eventually be removed permanently.[54] Instead of creating incentives for troubled immigrant families to find help, the new rules create the very likely possibility of splitting immigrant families apart. Many immigrant women may no doubt see the deportation of their abusive husbands as a tremendous incentive to report any instance of violence; however, in certain cases, a husband's criminal conviction for spousal abuse could conceivably result in the removal of *both* husband and wife, as well as their children, especially in instances where the wife's immigration status is dependent upon her husband's.[55] Because these rules tend to render the victims of domestic violence more vulnerable in these ways, the victims may well avoid the law altogether rather than seek help. For other immigrant women, the prospect of having a spouse deported may be enough to prevent their reporting or pursuing instances of domestic violence.

For many immigrant communities, the specter of mass removal has also altered local politics and long-standing community relations. In Lowell, Massachusetts, for instance, public officials welcomed the immigration rules of 1996 as a new set of powerful law enforcement tools. Local officials soon invited federal officials to begin deportation proceedings against Cambodian immigrants who had violated state laws and local ordinances. In November of 2002, the *Boston Globe* reported that "City leaders such as Mayor Rita Mercier and City Councilor Bud Caulfield…[saw] the proposal as an effective way of combating the city's gang violence, which exploded anew with deadly shootings last summer and largely afflicts its Southeast Asian and Latino populations."[56] Although many leaders in the Cambodian immigrant community sharply opposed this proposal, over a hundred Cambodian immigrants in Lowell were subsequently identified as removable aliens. A similar pattern of "law enforcement" could be found in other regions of the United States where Cambodian and Southeast Asian immigrants were concentrated, including Long Beach, California; Seattle, and in the Twin Cities region in Minnesota.[57]

Leading Southeast Asian community groups attempted to inform their immigrant constituents of these developments, but many of their efforts affirmed an overarching sense of fear and distance. The Southeast Asia Resource Action Center (SEARAC), based in Washington, D.C., recommended that immigrants seek American citizenship as the only protection against removal. However, "Southeast Asians who are not citizens, who have been convicted of a criminal offense, should seek counsel before applying for citizenship, traveling abroad, or taking any action that might attract INS attention."[58] Here was the essence of the anxiety created by the immigration law: in order to prevent banishment and exile, SEARAC and other similar organizations told immigrants and refugees to embrace American citizenship much more quickly; yet at the same time, they warned this same audience to approach with great caution, because the path to citizenship might surely lead to removal. These warnings appeared after and despite the Supreme Court's decision in *St. Cyr.*

Overall, the new rules governing removal have in these ways enhanced distinctions between citizens and non-citizens, especially in the criminal law, and they have instilled among immigrant communities new levels of anxiety that rest squarely on the possibility of being banished from the United States for minor crimes. Perhaps this is what Congressional leaders had intended in 1990 and 1996. The ease and speed with which a non-citizen could be removed under the new rules explain the tremendous rate of increase in overall deportations—removal based on criminal convictions alone have increased by about 700% since 1989. Many Congressional leaders and public officials have since lauded these trends, and have applauded the degree to which removal has become much more "efficient" under the new Department of Homeland Security. Officials charged with immigration enforcement recently reported that removal was becoming more "streamlined," that "inmates [are held] for less time before they're ultimately removed from the United States," and that this has been a "benefit to both" state and federal agencies.[59] The law was praised constantly for its efficiencies, despite severe costs imposed on immigrants, their families, or their communities.

CHAPTER 5

Toward Limits to Welfare and Family Reunification

SETTING THE FRAMEWORK

In the series of reports issued by President Bill Clinton's Commission on Immigration Reform, it became obvious that various members of the Commission were divided about how to deal with welfare benefits for immigrants, or the exact ordering of family reunification categories. The two issues were linked: several studies had suggested that many persons who had come under family reunification categories seemed disproportionately prone to rely on public assistance. Exactly what should be done to address this pattern remained a matter of considerable disagreement. In June of 1995, in the Commission's second series of published reports, the majority of members recommended modifying entire categories of family reunification visas, so as to exclude from these preference categories the adult unmarried sons and daughters of United States citizens, the adult married sons and daughters of permanent residents, the married sons and daughters of citizens, and siblings of United States citizens.

By rewriting these categories, immigration rules would strictly privilege the reunification of "nuclear families," not "extended families."[1] In her testimony to Congress, the Chair of the Commission, former House Representative Barbara Jordan, said that immigration policy ought to privilege "strong and intact nuclear families [because they are] the basic social unit consisting of parents and their dependent children living in one household." A majority of the Commission recommended that more-distant adult relatives should not be within the familiar preference categories, and that the sum of all family reunification visas — including those for immediate family members — should eventually be capped at 400,000 persons per year.[2]

Commissioner Warren Leiden, a leading immigration attorney who had been appointed by Democratic leaders in the House of Representatives, warned in a dissenting opinion that the majority's proposals moved the immigration law too far from its historic commitment to family reunification. Leiden argued that immigration rules should continue to support the reunification of adult sons and daughters of United States citizens. Moreover, Leiden said that the cap proposed by the majority was too low: under current projections, the cap should be set at about 535,000 family-reunification visas per year, so as to prevent chronic backlogs from forming across several sending countries, especially in Asia, Mexico, and Central America. Leiden concluded that if enacted, the majority's recommended changes would have eliminated or modified most of the provisions for family reunification in the Act of 1990, and that this would be a "short-sighted and rigid approach" to limiting legal immigration.[3]

At the heart of this issue was a recurring concern over the admission of "persons likely to become a public charge," borrowing the classic phrase from American immigration law in the 19th century. The underlying question was whether the United States should continue to bear some of the financial burdens associated with a broader commitment to family reunification. Barbara Jordan and a majority of the Commission did not favor just cutting off legal immigrants from public welfare programs, although they conceded that undocumented aliens should not receive most forms of public assistance. But in order to reduce the number of immigrants relying on public assistance *and* to preserve access to welfare programs to those who were admitted, the majority wanted to reduce the number of immigrants overall. By singling out "adults"—those who would not be the legal dependents of United States citizens or lawful permanent residents—the Commission sought to limit those family members most likely to rely on public assistance in the first place. After all, these persons were not admitted under the more stringent employment categories, and they were likely to be older and less malleable than younger immigrants.

The strategy was somewhat indirect, but the language of the Commission suggested precisely this approach: it noted, for example, "immigrants with relatively low education and skills may compete for jobs and public services with the most vulnerable of Americans, particularly those who are unemployed or underemployed," and that "elderly new immigrants are more likely to draw upon public services than elderly native-born Americans or immigrants who came to the United States at a younger age."[4]

As an astute student of migration patterns and trends, Commissioner Leiden probably knew of the additional costs associated with adult children or elderly parents, but he worried that a strategy of cutting off such persons "would be a tragic mistake," a form of discrimination analogous to Chinese Exclusion or Japanese American internment. Leiden said that the United States should reaffirm a commitment to family reunification for all classes of persons, especially in a nation devoted to "social and political equality." Leiden even suggested diverting other categories of admission — namely diversity visas and unused employment visas — toward family reunification.[5]

As contentious as this issue had become in 1995, the Commission had reached consensus a year earlier on another related set of policies designed also to reduce the "costs" of poorer immigrants. Specifically, the Commission wanted to tie family sponsors and immigrant beneficiaries closer together financially, by requiring "affidavits of support [to] be legally enforceable." "Mechanisms should be developed that would ensure that sponsors actually provide the support they have promised." Moreover, the Commission said: "A serious effort to enhance and enforce the public charge provisions in immigration law is needed to ensure that legal immigrants do not require public assistance within five years of entry for reasons that existed prior to entry." To protect social welfare programs, persons likely to be a public charge should be more aggressively excluded, and persons who have become a public charge within five years of their entry should be removed.[6] Commissioner Leiden did not object formally to these policy recommendations in 1994 or 1995, but in a hearing on Capitol Hill in 2001, four years after the Commission had dissolved, he regretted how these policies were having a negative and regrettable impact on family reunification.[7]

PERSONAL RESPONSIBILITY: "THE PRINCIPLE OF SELF-SUFFICIENCY"

At the beginning of Title IV, a portion of the Personal Responsibility and Work Opportunity Reconciliation Act of 1996, or "PRWORA" (hereafter the Welfare Act of 1996), Congress presented "Statements of National Policy Concerning Welfare and Immigration," which read as a kind of preamble to the new set of rules governing welfare and immigrants. The statute reiterated much of what the Commission on Immigration Reform had stated in its final published report in 1997. This new law was passed within a few weeks of the Anti-Terrorism Act, and both rules shared some of the same legislative sponsors.[8]

The Welfare Act promised to reform the entire structure of public assistance, and it specifically dealt with immigrants' eligibility for a wide range of government programs. Again, the new law reflected concerns in a series of scholarly papers and government reports published in the late 1980s and 1990s that showed that immigrants relied on public assistance at higher rates than American citizens; congressional testimony included references to these studies, as well as separate instances where local officials confirmed high rates of welfare use in many specific regions.[9] Jane Ross, a researcher at the General Accounting Office, reported to the Senate in February 1996 that the proportion of non-citizens relying on federal and state supplemental security income doubled from 1986 to 1994, that non-citizens received about $4 billion in such income transfers in 1995, and that about 46% of all non-citizen recipients applied for these programs within four years of entering the United States.[10]

Congress's own statements in Title IV insisted that American immigration rules had always attempted to prohibit such dependency, and to demand that newcomers support themselves financially. Yet "despite the principle of self-sufficiency, aliens have been applying for and receiving public benefits from Federal, State, and Local governments at increasing rates." Sponsors of immigrants were not living up to promises of supporting their immigrant beneficiaries, and immigrant beneficiaries themselves too easily relied on welfare.[11] By phrasing the issue in this way, Congress then presented some of the most severe restrictions on welfare eligibility for non-citizens in the Welfare Act of 1996.

In public, some legislative sponsors, including the Republican representative Jay Kim, a first-generation Korean immigrant, said that Congress should have gone even further. Kim himself had suggested a rule in 1994 that would have denied federal disaster relief aid to illegal aliens; Kim had also supported the passage of Proposition 187 in his native California in 1994.[12] For many commentators, the Welfare Act *was* a federal variant of Proposition 187.

Indeed, the anger built over immigration reform had been brewing for some time. Other bills were just as harsh, and were born of the same hostility toward immigrants prevalent in the political climate of the early 1990s. In one bill sponsored in 1993, Republicans like Richard Shelby of Alabama and Democrats like Harry Reid of Nevada joined in support of a rule to cap indefinitely all immigration to fewer than 300,000 persons per year.[13] The Republican representative from Texas, Lamar Smith, proposed another immigration bill in 1995 that was inspired by the Jordan

Commission, a bill that would have reduced legal immigration by about a third, mostly by changing or limiting the second, third, and fourth family reunification preferences in the Act of 1990.[14] These proposals would have eliminated large numbers of potential immigrants entirely.

While the Welfare Act did not limit the numbers of persons entering per se, it changed the rules under which immigrants could enter under the current ceilings and floors retained from the Act of 1990. The Welfare Act represented a compromise of sorts—despite its harsh provisions, it represented a political middle in the spectrum of options weighed in Congress for about ten years. It was premised on qualitative immigration criteria, although its supporters no doubt expected quantitative reductions as well. Support for an immigration and a welfare compromise was overwhelming: President Bill Clinton signed the Welfare Act in August of 1996, fulfilling his campaign promise to end "welfare as we know it."[15]

In terms of welfare policy, this new rule meant that the federal government would severely limit the number of years a person could rely on public assistance, the theory being that welfare should act only as a temporary buffer in hard times, but not become a "way of life." Furthermore, the congressional discussions of welfare policy clearly tied welfare dependency to single motherhood and irresponsible parenting, especially the neglect of fathers for the economic welfare of their children.[16] In Title I of the Welfare Act, Congress listed these findings about the American family: "Marriage is the foundation of a successful society. Marriage is an essential institution of a successful society which promotes the interests of children. Promotion of responsible fatherhood and motherhood is integral to successful child rearing and the well-being of children."[17] Additional findings included observations about increasing rates of teen pregnancy, increasing numbers of women having children out of wedlock, and increasing rates of poverty among both classes of persons. Some findings were presented dryly, without much elaboration: "The absence of a father in the life of a child has a negative effect on school performance and peer adjustment," for example. Thematically, the focus of the Welfare Act was on renewing a sense of responsibility to reverse the disintegration of the traditional family, typified by the teenage mother, the unwed mother, and the absent father.[18]

The analogy to immigrants and immigration proceeded in this way: if the problem for American citizens was that parents were acting irresponsibly with respect to their children, the problem for immigrant families was that the sponsors of immigrant beneficiaries were too often negligent of their duties to support family members. In addition, the law suggested, immigrants themselves were too financially irresponsible by becoming so dependent upon welfare.

The provisions of the Welfare Act that determine eligibility for public benefits for non-citizens are outlined in Table 5.1. The most obvious change lay in the substantial discretion given to the individual states in determining welfare eligibility, which marked a turn toward "devolution," where the federal government would share welfare costs with states, but the states themselves could largely determine who can and cannot participate in public assistance programs.[19] This devolution was not an entirely new concept—the federal government had given states block grants for in-kind public assistance, and then allowed states to determine eligibility. But under Supreme Court decisions like *Graham v. Richardson* in 1971, states were prohibited from denying all non-citizens access to these types of programs; these past rulings relied, in part, on the theory that matters of immigration and immigration status were within federal, not state, jurisdiction. The new Welfare Act listed obvious discriminations against non-citizens as major distinct features of *federal* law, thus immunizing them from similar constitutional challenges.[20]

Indeed, portions of the Welfare Act *required* states to discriminate against various classes of non-immigrants. A section of the Act set definitions for "qualified aliens" for purposes of testing welfare eligibility. To be "qualified," an alien must have been admitted lawfully as one of the following: a permanent resident; an asylee; or a refugee. Qualified aliens can also include persons paroled into the United States for at least one year, persons granted conditional entry, and persons granted cancellation of removal.[21] Anyone not a qualified alien—especially an illegal immigrant—could not be eligible forthwith for any public assistance program funded all or in part by the federal government. On the one hand, devolution meant greater control by the states; on the other hand, new federal definitions of eligibility restricted states from being more generous. Even if some states wanted to extend benefits to "unqualified aliens," they could not.

Furthermore, the Welfare Act reduced overall the numbers of immigrants eligible for welfare. For example, sponsors and immigrant beneficiaries were tied closely together under other provisions of the Act: "the income and resources" of sponsors and their spouses are deemed to be available to their immigrant beneficiary for purposes of determining social welfare eligibility.[22] By including the entire family's household income to determine whether an immigrant beneficiary was eligible for welfare, far fewer immigrants would be so eligible. Defining "qualified aliens" narrowly, and then treating them and their sponsoring families as one unit

TABLE 5.1 Alien Eligibility for Selected Federal Programs under the Welfare Act of 1996

	SSI	Food Stamps	Medicaid	TANF
Immigrants				
Entered before 8/22/96	If on rolls 8/22/96 or subsequently disabled	Yes, if 65 or over by 8/26/96, subsequently disabled, or while under 18	Yes, for SSI-derivative benefits or emergency services. Otherwise, state option	State option
First five years after 8/22/96	No	No	Emergency only	No
After five years in the U.S.	No	No	Yes, for SSI-derivative benefits or emergency services, otherwise, state option	State option
Refugees and Asylees				
First five years after entry or asylum	Yes	Yes	Yes	Yes
After five years in the U.S.	Yes, for 2 more years	Yes, for 2 more years	Yes, for 2 more years and for emergency services, otherwise, state option.	State Option
Non-immigrants and Undocumented Aliens	No	No	Emergency only	No

Source: *Joyce Vialet*, Alien Eligibility for Public Assistance (Congressional Research Service, 96-617 EPW, 1998).

under the "deeming" provisions, the Welfare Act severely curtailed the numbers of non-citizens who could receive public benefits. Initial estimates thus gauged the scope of the new Act: literally, hundreds of thousands of refugees and immigrants would lose eligibility.[23] According to one study, because so many immigrants would lose access to these benefits, the federal government would realize substantial savings in the near future:

> The total cost savings to the federal government from reduced eligibility for immigrants are estimated at $20–25 billion for the six-year period between 1997 and 2002. This is approximately 45% of the projected $54 billion savings from the entire welfare reform bill. 85% of these reduced outlays arise from SSI, food stamps, AFDC, and Medicaid.[24]

Ending welfare as we know it came at a very high price for permanent residents. Early critics decried these rules as "excessive and unfair." As noted above, even the Commission on Immigration Reform opposed these types of sweeping changes governing access to public assistance for legal immigrants. President Clinton himself subsequently criticized Title IV of the Welfare Act, promising to repeal some of these provisions upon his reelection in November of 1996. Rudolph Giuliani, then Mayor of New York, described Title IV as "inhumane and indecent," and promised "to file a separate suit challenging those provisions of the welfare law that deny public services to legal immigrants."[25] Subsequent reforms were passed in Congress for legal immigrants who had been in the United States before the passage of the Welfare Act, though they did nothing for new immigrants arriving to the United States after 1996.

A LEGALLY ENFORCEABLE CONTRACT: THE NEW AFFIDAVITS OF SUPPORT

Enacted a month after the Welfare Act, the Illegal Immigration Reform and Immigrant Responsibility Act of 1996 (mentioned earlier in Chapter 4) continued the same themes found in its predecessor. The Responsibility Act enacted two key recommendations from the President's Commission on Immigration Reform: Title V of the Responsibility Act provided for specific criteria for excluding persons likely to become a public charge, and then required a binding contract between sponsors and the federal government in which the former agreed to be financially liable for any public services that their immigrant beneficiaries might consume. This responsibility would last until the immigrant became a naturalized citizen, or until the immigrant had worked for forty qualifying quarters under the

Social Security Act, which would be ten years at the earliest. As much as immigrants were "deemed" financially linked to their sponsors under the Welfare Act, the Responsibility Act extended the period for which sponsors and immigrant beneficiaries would remain so attached.

The Responsibility Act reframed the public charge provision that had remained an essential feature of American immigration law. In the first part of the public charge provision, Congress authorized immigration officials to assess all immigrants under these five criteria: age; health; family status; assets, resources, and financial status; and education and skills.[26] Moreover, any alien admitted as an immigrant for family reunification or for employment had to file the new affidavit of support, defined as a "contract" and deliberately so, to overrule the principle that had first been articulated in *Renel*. The terms of the contract required that "the sponsor agrees to provide support to maintain the sponsored alien at an annual income that is not less than 125 percent of the Federal poverty line during the period in which the affidavit is enforceable." The contract "is legally enforceable against the sponsor by the sponsored alien, the Federal Government, any State (or any political subdivision of such State), or by any other entity that provides any means-tested public benefit ... consistent with the provisions of this section."[27] Any time an immigrant consumes any public benefit, the entity providing the benefit may send the sponsor a bill, thus enforcing the terms of the affidavit. If sponsors do not pay, they expose themselves to a range of civil lawsuits, as well as fines up to $5,000.[28] Curiously, the immigrant relatives who were sponsored may sue their own sponsor for financial support to pay for or to avoid the cost of public assistance.

The Responsibility Act also set a minimum threshold for persons wishing to sponsor an immigrant beneficiary. Under these provisions, the sponsors needed to prove affirmatively that they themselves were not public charges, or likely to become so. A sponsor must be "a citizen or national of the United States or an alien who is lawfully admitted to the United States for permanent residence; is at least 18 years of age; is domiciled in any of the several States of the United States, the District of Columbia, or any territory or possession of the United States; is petitioning for the admission of the alien under §204 [for family re-unification visas]; and demonstrates ... the means to maintain an annual income equal to at least 125 percent of the Federal poverty line."

That figure worked out to about $20,000 per year for a family of four. Sponsors who failed this income test on their own could find another co-sponsor, although that additional sponsor would be liable, too, for any public services consumed by the immigrant beneficiary. To determine whether a sponsor was financially eligible, Congress wanted hard proof: "For purposes of this section, a demonstration of the means to maintain income shall include provision of a certified copy of the individual's Federal income tax return for the individual's three most recent taxable years and a written statement, executed under oath or as permitted under penalty of perjury...that the copies are certified copies of such returns." Sponsors were also required to show proof of their Social Security Number, which would be kept on file with the Attorney General.[29]

The income provisions of the Responsibility Act were likely to disqualify large groups of immigrants. A study commissioned by the Urban Institute a year after the Act suggested that about one quarter to one third of the five million immigrants who entered between 1980 and 1985 would fail the income test.[30] The Immigration and Naturalization Service itself suggested that "roughly half of immigrants from Mexico and El Salvador, one-third of Dominicans and Koreans, and one-quarter of Chinese and Jamaicans could not have met the new income requirement for sponsoring family members."[31]

Indeed, this set of rules was devastating for poorer families seeking to reunite in the United States. Though American immigration rules had been relatively mindful of family relationships, these "reforms" now subjected family sponsors to tremendous financial liabilities, so much so that the only likely outcome was to discourage family reunification. Congress had overruled court decisions like *Renel*, which had had the force of law for over forty years, in a rather straightforward way. Congress rejected the idea that an affidavit of support constituted only a "moral obligation," and Congress recreated the affidavit as a binding contract involving sponsors, immigrants, and government agencies providing public assistance.

Some critics charged that these reforms were "reactionary," and many pinned the blame for these policies strictly upon the conservative majority in Congress. However, as dramatic as this change was, it clearly had bipartisan support by 1996. When Dan Stein, the Executive Director for the Federation for American Immigration Reform (FAIR) testified to the Senate, he insisted that "the American people are uniformly in support of restoring the meaning and enforceability of the affidavits of support."[32] FAIR itself had long been supportive of efforts to limit immigration to the United States in general, particularly because its members felt that immigrants were straining public resources, including public assistance programs; it was one of several "leading restrictionist groups" that had been active throughout the 1980s and 1990s to promote restrictions on welfare programs for legal immigrants.[33]

But by 1996, even liberal organizations were conceding the need to enforce some kind of support agreement between immigrant sponsors and beneficiaries, and to include "deeming" provisions in assessing welfare eligibility. In 1995, Karen Narasaki, the Executive Director for the National Asian Pacific American Legal Consortium, said in her own testimony to the House that while "other proposed changes go too far"—especially the proposed elimination of entire categories of family reunification visas, or the removal of most legal immigrants from public assistance programs—"the Consortium supports the concept of making affidavits of support legally enforceable." Narasaki suggested that other leading Asian American civil rights groups shared the same position, especially among the most active affiliates of the Consortium, which included Asian American Legal Defense and Education Fund in New York, the Asian Law Caucus in San Francisco, and the Asian Pacific Legal Center of Southern California in Los Angeles.[34]

Democratic officials were more likely to support these changes in policy rather than simply acquiesce. For instance, Mary Jo Bane, a leading scholar of poverty and welfare policy and a key official in the Department of Health and Human Services, said in her own testimony in May of 1996 that the Clinton Administration supported binding affidavits of support between sponsors and immigrant beneficiaries.[35] Karen Darner, a Democrat in the Virginia House of Delegates, also spoke on behalf of the National Conference of State Legislatures in favor of a binding affidavit: "If sponsors agree to provide financial support for an immigrant, they ought to honor their promise and be held accountable if they leave the immigrant in the lurch."[36] Bane and Darner also expressed strong support for the "deeming" provisions that would eventually appear in the Welfare Act of 1996. It may have been true that these changes in law were hard on poorer immigrants and their sponsoring families, and they could appear in that way as anti-immigrant in essence, but it would be untrue to say that these rules were supported only by a restrictionist reactionary fringe in Congress.

RESTORING (SOME) SUPPORT

The passage of the Welfare Act in late 1996 caused a wave of panic throughout many immigrant communities in the United States. In response to their pending removal from public assistance programs, immigrants and immigrants' right groups protested the provisions of the Welfare Act throughout the following year. Busloads of immigrants from San Francisco traveled to Sacramento, carrying banners that said "Why Are You Killing Me?" and "Don't Punish Immigrants." Reports of immigrants protesting the cuts in welfare ranged from Los Angeles, St. Paul, and New York, including vocal actions by Vietnamese, Hmong, Russian, Bolivian, Mexican, and Korean immigrants.[37] In January, Hmong immigrants testified to Congress about the hardships likely to befall them after a sudden cut in public assistance.[38]

In the spring of 1997, the late Democratic Senator from Minnesota, Paul Wellstone, proposed a measure in the Senate to restore benefits to immigrants, effectively overruling Title IV of the Welfare Act.[39] In March, the American Civil Liberties Union, the National Asian Pacific American Legal Consortium, and a coalition of other immigrant and civil rights groups filed class-action lawsuits in San Francisco and New York to render the Welfare Act unconstitutional, in part for denying disability aid to disabled, blind, and elderly immigrants.[40] In April, "the Union of Councils for Soviet Jews, the National Asian Pacific American Legal Consortium, and organizations representing Kurdish and Bosnian refugees [held] a protest rally outside at the U.S. Capitol," followed two days later by "a reception for members of Congress with elderly immigrants as the featured speakers."[41]

Shortly thereafter, prominent Republican senators replied to Wellstone's proposed repeal, opting instead to restore benefits to persons already receiving them at the time that the Welfare Act was passed. Joined by eight Republicans in the House, Senators John Chafee of Rhode Island, Alfonse D'Amato of New York, and Mike DeWine of Ohio suggested that "restoration of benefits [was] a matter of fairness to poor, elderly, and disabled immigrants who came here under one set of rules, only to have them changed years later." Republican governors George Pataki of New York and Jim Edgar of Illinois warned that any impending cuts in federal programs would unfairly shift public assistance burdens to the states.[42] Southeast Asian American organizations such as the Lao Veterans and the Lao Family from Minnesota coordinated the efforts of hundreds of Hmong refugees impacted by the new law. The heavy involvement of Southeast Asian immigrants was largely due to the fact that these immigrants more than others were likely to rely on public assistance programs; nevertheless, the degree to which they achieved political organization and the passion with which they waged an effort to change American law were impressive.[43]

These efforts produced another legislative compromise. The Welfare Act was amended to soften the blow to immigrants, as Bill Clinton had promised in his last Presidential campaign. Provisions in the Balanced Budget Act of 1997 and the Non-Citizen Benefit Clarification Act of 1998 said that portions of the Welfare Act "shall not apply to eligibility for benefits [for the supplemental social security income program], or to eligibility for benefits under any other program that is based on eligibility for benefits under the program so defined, for an alien who was receiving such benefits on August 22, 1996."[44] The Republican reply to Wellstone and Clinton represented again a political middle in the fight over welfare and immigration. While these provisions did relieve the burden for immigrants already in the United States, it did not repeal the portions of the Welfare Act that determined eligibility for new immigrants and refugees. New arrivals were still barred for up to ten years, and refugees and asylees had to move off public assistance after seven. Moreover, there was mounting evidence that many immigrants who might have been eligible for public assistance were avoiding state and federal programs for fear of adverse immigration consequences. Because of the new and more aggressive public charge provisions in the Act, many immigrants were right to be afraid.

After 1998, subsequent research on welfare participation rates showed that the Welfare Act did have a dramatic impact on non-citizens. A recent study by George Borjas, an immigration specialist at Harvard and a leading intellectual proponent of the welfare and immigration reform legislation in 1996, concluded that welfare participation fell precipitously among immigrant households after the Welfare Act, especially in California, which had the highest population of immigrants of any state. The Welfare Act had an initial chilling effect, "either by making some immigrant households ineligible for receiving some types of assistance, or by mistakenly raising concerns among eligible immigrant households that receiving welfare could have adverse repercussions on their immigration status (and perhaps lead to deportation)." However, after the states began implementing policies in accordance with the principle of devolution in the Act, many states, including California, chose to retain fairly generous state-sponsored safety nets for immigrant households: "The fact that some states chose to offer a state-funded safety net to their immigrant populations helped cushion the impact of federal welfare reform."[45] For Professor Borjas, this trend may have been unduly influenced by the political participation of the immigrants who were themselves the object of welfare reform: "The possibility that the immigrants themselves altered the political equilibrium in these states is worrisome, and raises doubts about the wisdom of granting states the right to enhance the benefits that are available to immigrants."[46]

Pressured by elderly, blind, and disabled immigrants, by Hmong allies who fought on behalf of the Americans in Laos, and by the specter of immigrant children going hungry, federal and state officials were prone to undo the harshest of rules, while the states increased their own public assistance programs to make up for lost federal support. For economists like Borjas, who had long lamented welfare dependency among immigrants, this trend was not a good thing:

> It seems ... that the American people do not wish to bear political, social, and economic costs of removing immigrants already in the United States from the welfare rolls. It is naïve, after all, to assume that there are no long-run consequences from denying needy immigrants access to food stamps or medical services. In the end, it is probably easier and cheaper to address the problem raised by the immigration of public charges not by 'ending welfare as we know it,' but by reforming immigration policy instead.[47]

Borjas suggested that the true key to limiting immigrants' access to welfare was to limit immigrants, not their access to public services *after* they had been admitted.

In a way, it was as though the original problem of immigration and welfare reform were coming full circle: perhaps it would have been best, according to Borjas, to have pressed the reframing of family reunification preferences, especially to limit the arrival of adult immigrants into the country, rather than rely on welfare reform. It would be better, he had suggested, if fewer of the poor would come; the obvious groups for elimination were indeed those adult family members of citizens and permanent residents. But eliminating these family reunification categories had been the primary cause of the long-standing rift within the President's Commission on Immigration Reform. After all, that was why Commissioner Warren Leiden wrote his impassioned dissent to retain the family-reunification preferences against Barbara Jordan's majority opinion to limit these paths into the United States. In his scholarly articles in 2002, George Borjas might have regretted that Barbara Jordan had not ultimately prevailed in that argument.

PATTERNS OF FAMILY REUNIFICATION SINCE 1996

It is still too early to measure accurately and completely the full impact of the Welfare Act and the Responsibility Act on patterns of family reunification. It is even more difficult to assess this impact in light of the recent historic events of September 11th, and the subsequent political developments that have collectively reframed immigration law once again. Family migration itself occurs along several complex variables, and the decision that family members make to reunite in the United States is one of the most complex phenomena in immigration studies.[48] As dramatic as the

Welfare Act and the Responsibility Act were, no one can say for certain how these rules directly impacted the migration patterns of immigrant families.[49]

However, preliminary statistical analyses of government figures do suggest that family-based migration has now become a much smaller fraction of total migration to the United States. Generally, figures for family-sponsored immigration under the four preference categories can fluctuate substantially from year to year: in 1995, for example, family-sponsored immigration under the four preference categories numbered 238,122 persons. In 1996, it reached 294,174 persons, the highest it has ever been since then. Those figures fell by more than a third in the first two years after the Responsibility and Welfare Acts were enacted into law—213,331 persons in 1997 and 191,480 persons in 1998. That is, in 1998, about 102,694 fewer persons were coming to the United States as immigrants under family reunification preferences.[50] It would be tempting to see these figures alone as profound evidence of a dampening effect on family reunification caused by the rules passed in 1996. Much more careful research is still needed, however, to see whether the rules by themselves had such dramatic effects, or whether this pattern was caused by another variable or by a combination of variables.

Family-based immigration is still a significant fraction of all immigration to the United States, but the trends have clearly favored nuclear families. In 1999, total family-sponsored immigration under the four preferences of the Act of 1990 rose slightly to 216,883 persons, then to over 230,000 persons per year in 2000 and 2001. Last year, only 187,069 persons were admitted as immigrants under family reunification preferences. Throughout this period, the number of persons admitted as the immediate relatives of United States citizens fluctuated as well, from about 300,000 persons in 1996, to a low of 258,584 persons in 1999, then to the current peak of 485,960 persons in 2002.[51] If the whole point of immigration reform in the early 1990s was to limit or to reduce the number of poorer, older family members reuniting in the United States, then it would seem that the rules in 1996 probably did have some effect on this goal: under the current set of laws, immediate nuclear family members are much more likely to reunite than older relatives or extended kin. One can easily speculate that the entire set of rules—the threshold requirements to become a sponsor, the deeming provisions, the affidavits of support, and the public charge provisions—all worked to provide formidable disincentives for all immigrant families, and especially poorer immigrant families, from seeking family reunification. Even for families that did petition for reunification, the new rules will no doubt raise considerable anxieties,

TABLE 5.2 Family and Employment-Based Migration, Selected Years

Year	Total immigrants admitted	Quota Immigrants	Family-based Preferences	Employment-based Preferences	Percent employment-based quota immigrants
Table A/All Immigrants					
1985	570,009	264,152	213,257	50,895	19%
1995	720,461	323,458	238,122	85,336	26%
2002	1,063,732	362,037	187,069	174,968	48%
Table B/Immigrants from Asia					
1995	267,931	132,236	84,177	48,059	36%
2002	342,099	175,350	68,287	107,063	61%

Source: INS Statistical Yearbooks (1985, 1995, and 2002).

because if the immigrant beneficiary becomes indigent within the next ten years, it could prove an economic disaster to the sponsor as well as the immigrant beneficiary. For these reasons, we believe that the downward pattern of family reunification within the preference categories will most likely continue for the foreseeable future, especially in light of recent test cases demanding the enforcement of those affidavits.[52]

More instructive than the sheer decline of family reunification visas are the comparisons between family reunification and employment-based admissions into the United States since 1996. The number of employment-based visas also fluctuates substantially from year to year, but the total fraction of employment-based visas has shown consistent increases from year to year, especially from 1995 to 2002. Table 5.2 shows some of these numbers from 1985, 1995, and 2002, both in the aggregate and for immigrants from Asia. In 1985, of all immigrants who were admitted into the United States under both family reunification and employment-based visas, persons in the latter category constituted 19% of the total. By 1995, five years after the Act of 1990 increased employment-based visas to 140,000 per year, the fraction of employment-based visas rose to 26%. By 2002, immigrants admitted under employment-based preferences were admitted at about the same rate as immigrants coming under family reunification preferences. The trend among Asian immigrants was even more pronounced: in 1995, 36% of Asian immigrants admitted under the preference categories were coming under the employment preferences; by 2002, an amazing 61% of all Asian immigrants were admitted under employment preference categories.

These figures—as striking as they are—do not capture adequately the shift in migration trends toward employment and away from family reunification, especially among Asian immigrants. In the next chapters, we discuss recent immigration laws that have brought hundreds of thousands of highly skilled Asian professionals to the United States since 1998. Because these laws draw to the United States persons who are "non-immigrants," or persons who in theory will not remain in the United States as permanent residents or as citizens, the laws and trends are illuminating for how they use predominantly Asian workers to maximize efficiencies in American law, economy, and society.

PART **III**
The Highly Skilled

CHAPTER 6

"Temporary Workers" in American Law and Society Since 1990

ADVERSE EFFECTS: THE DEVELOPMENT OF NON-IMMIGRANT VISAS

One of the most dramatic changes in immigration trends over the last fifteen years has been the explosive growth of "non-immigrants" coming into the United States under various employment categories. As mentioned in the last chapter, non-immigrants are people who typically do not intend to stay in the United States: in late 19th-century immigration law, they were tourists, students, or merchants. Even the Chinese Exclusion Act exempted such classes of Chinese persons from exclusion, largely because they were "temporary," and because they would leave after conducting affairs considered mutually beneficial for both them and the United States. Chinese merchants were especially accorded deference in the law, for even in the midst of race-based exclusion, federal judges noted that "commerce with China is of the greatest value, and is constantly increasing," such that immigration officials ought to avoid "unnecessary and embarrassing restrictions" against Chinese merchants.[1]

The Immigration and Nationality Act of 1952 provided for non-immigrant workers under §101(a)(15)(H)(i), dividing them generally into three categories: professionals and persons in "specialty" occupations (H-1); persons performing services unavailable in the United States (H-2); and industrial trainees (H-3). People entering under the H-3 have never constituted a significant group; there were just over 3,200 persons in 2002.

The other two H visas have been extremely contentious, each with distinct histories, and both have been difficult to implement with any degree of political consensus or cooperation. In almost all instances, employers hiring temporary non-immigrant workers have had to show that the domestic labor force was either non-existent or inadequate, and that the hiring of non-immigrants would be in no way "harmful" to the interests of domestic laborers. The rules for obtaining H non-immigrant visas have developed in a way that they are now more consonant with the rules governing permanent employment visas: that is, the legal grounds for gaining temporary admission have become almost the same as those for permanent residency. In fact, as we shall see, because many persons admitted under the H visas are so similar to those admitted as immigrants under employment categories, these "non-immigrants" frequently adjust into permanent residency.

Class position and educational background often determine which person gets an H-2 or an H-1 non-immigrant visa. For example, those admitted under the H-2 have typically included agricultural workers, mostly in seasonal employment. This visa has had a complicated and terrible history tied to the Bracero Programs throughout the 1940s, which "imported" thousands of Mexican farm workers to the United States. Ernesto Galaraza, Juan Ramon Garcia, and Kitty Calavita have all written about various facets of the Bracero Program, and all show how profoundly exploitative and unjust this system was.[2] The Act of 1952 retained a version of the Program to meet the purported labor needs of growers in the Southwest. The new law, however, required employers to show that they could not find domestic workers to fill these positions, and that the hiring of these seasonal workers would not depress wages or working conditions. In large part because of these requirements, agricultural employers mostly ignored the law, hiring undocumented laborers instead of procuring "legitimate" seasonal workers. Nonetheless, the Immigration Reform and Control Act of 1986 reaffirmed these requirements and then split the H-2 into two categories—the H-2A for agricultural workers, and the H-2B for non-agricultural workers, particularly those in relatively low-wage unskilled labor for which there was "a shortage of American workers."

Persons under H-2As still worked in agriculture, and people under H-2Bs have worked in industries ranging from vegetable packing to slaughterhouses. Altogether, under the H-2, those with "lesser skills" have constituted a significant number of entrants that has grown every year, from about 25,000 in 1985 to 100,000 in 2001. Most come from Mexico, Central America, and the Caribbean—especially Jamaica.

But again, the rule itself is mostly ignored. Many, many more people who *should be* H-2s are undocumented aliens, largely because the Act of 1986 increased the threshold requirements for employers seeking these types of temporary workers. Although the Act of 1986 attempted to "streamline" the procedures for procuring these visas, agricultural employers and others have simply sidestepped the rule, despite new penalties in the law that targeted employers who knowingly hired undocumented workers.[3] Some have said that the visas were not worth the trouble because of the bureaucratic hassles in obtaining labor certification (showing that the non-immigrant workers who will be hired will not have an adverse impact on domestic workers), and chiefly because undocumented aliens are so readily available to work. Even though, for the first time in 2001, H-2Bs exceeded the original cap of 66,000 persons per year set in the Act of 1986, the number who *should be* H-2As and H-2Bs far exceed the 100,000 persons entering under both categories in fiscal year 2001. They represent those in the lower and lowest echelons of the American economy, and in many instances, they are part of the "invisible economy" of transient, seasonal undocumented workers. Estimates of the population of undocumented aliens in the United States are notoriously inaccurate for obvious reasons, but they range in the millions. Most are from Mexico, South America, and Central America, as well as Asia, and they work in occupations that ought to be covered under the H-2 visas.[4]

The most contentious non-immigrant visa, and the most important avenue for employment-based Asian migration, has been the H-1 visa. Since 1952, persons entering under the H-1 had included medical professionals, especially nurses, who had come in fairly large numbers to meet the chronic shortage of medical professionals in American hospitals. But people in this group were also a more varied lot: they included athletes, entertainers, even fashion models. As to why some of them were even "professionals" or performing in "specialty occupations" wasn't always clear. The fuzziness of this H-1 category and the perceived abuses of the H-1 visas moved Congress to amend the law in 1989 and 1990, under the Immigration Nursing Relief Act of 1989 and the Immigration Act of 1990. The Act of 1990 fundamentally changed all non-immigrant visas related to employment in the United States, with the most profound effect on the H-1.

First, under the rule in 1989, Congress provided special avenues for non-immigrant nurses to adjust status toward permanent residency. Many had been in H-1 status for several years, and because many had had difficulty adjusting under regular channels—in part because so many came from Asian countries with horrific backlogs—Congress provided them with this "relief." According to Enid Trucios-Haynes, a law professor at the

University of Louisville, "approximately 75% of the non-citizen nurses at the time were from the Philippines. For this national origin group, at that time, the wait for an employment based visa for permanent residence could exceed ten years."[5] The Act of 1989 facilitated their adjustments of status into permanent residency by removing them from the queue for employment-based visas—provided that they had been working "for at least 3 years before the date of application for adjustment of status (whether or not before, on, or after, the date of the enactment of this Act)," and "[have] been employed as a registered nurse in the United States."[6]

Then, conversely, Congress made it *more difficult* for subsequent foreign nurses to gain admission as non-immigrant workers in the United States. This appeared in a revised §101(a)(15)(H)(i)(a); the last letter, (a), accounts for the creation of the H-1A visa especially for registered nurses. The 1989 rule was an important precursor to the 1990 rule: in spelling out the requirements for new non-immigrant nurses, the law demanded that all non-immigrant nurses be fully certified and trained according to the standards set by the hospitals wishing to employ them.

Moreover, when the hospitals petitioned the INS for a non-immigrant visa on behalf of the foreign nurse, the hospital had to overcome several important burdens: they needed to show to the Department of Labor that "the employment of the alien will not adversely affect the wages and working conditions of registered nurses similarly employed"; that "the alien will be paid the wage rate for registered nurses similarly employed by the facility"; and that the hospital "has taken and is taking timely and significant steps designed to recruit and retain sufficient registered nurses who are United States citizens or immigrants who are authorized to perform nursing services, in order to remove as quickly as reasonably possible the dependence of the facility on nonimmigrant registered nurses." Finally, American nurses and their unions had to be notified of the impending hire of a non-immigrant nurse—this notification suggested a kind of veto for any nurse or nursing union that perceived itself harmed by the hiring of foreigners.[7] Overall, the new requirements suggested that foreign nurses should be hired only as a necessary evil, a last resort when the domestic labor market had truly failed.[8]

SKILLED WORKERS IN SPECIALTY OCCUPATIONS: THE H-1B VISA IN THE ACT OF 1990

The Immigration Act of 1990 reframed the H-1B to encompass immigrants working on projects for the "Department of Defense," "fashion models," and those in "specialty occupations." Persons entering under the first two descriptions have never constituted a significant number of H-1B admissions. In general, "specialty occupations" are ones that "require: (a) a theoretical and practical application of a body of highly specialized knowledge, and (b) attainment of a bachelor's or higher degree in the specific specialty (or its equivalent) as a minimum for entry into the occupation in the United States."[9] In addition, employers hiring H-1B employees must submit to the Department of Labor proof of the following:

> That [the employer] (i) is offering and will offer during the period of authorized employment to aliens and to other individuals employed in the occupational classification and in the area of employment wages that are at least—(I) the actual wage level for the occupational classification at the place of employment, or (II) the prevailing wage level for the occupational classification in the area of employment, whichever is greater, determined as of the time of filing the application, and (ii) will provide working conditions for such aliens that will not adversely affect the working conditions of workers similarly employed.[10]

The law provided several penalties for employers who wanted to sidestep these requirements; these penalties would most obviously be inflicted when similarly situated American citizen employees reported the unlawful hiring of cheap foreign labor. "The employer shall make available for public examination, within one working day after the date on which an [H-1B] application ... is filed, at the employer's principal place of business or worksite, a copy of each such application (and accompanying documentation)."[11] Again, domestic employees were given a veto of sorts, and the hiring of non-immigrants would appear possible only when it becomes a necessity.

From fiscal year 1991 until the end of the fiscal year 1998, the cap for H-1B visas had been set at 65,000 persons, and all non-immigrants under the H-1B could remain in the United States for no more than six years—an initial three-year visa that could be renewed for an additional three years.[12] But in terms of their legal status, the one significant advantage for H-1B non-immigrants was that they could also seek permanent residency in the United States even as they were working here "temporarily." Now they could have "dual intent" prior to entry, rather than having to declare that they were only here temporarily as a necessary condition for obtaining H-1B status. This was an important change, one that was often an overlooked feature of the Act of 1990, but which tended to blur the line between "temporary" and "permanent" workers in the American economy.[13]

In many ways, hiring a skilled foreign worker under the H-1B became a substantial chore, even more than hiring an H-2: in attempting to get an

H-1B approved through the INS, the employer became the formal "petitioner," the worker the "beneficiary." Before the petition could be filed, the employer had to define the beneficiary's job title and duties, where the job could be found in the Dictionary of Occupational Titles (which is a massive tome published by the Department of Labor), the minimum education and experience required for the job, and the place where the beneficiary would work. All of these were used to determine a "prevailing wage," the wage commonly paid for persons in *that* type of job, in *that* region, with *that* level of experience and education. Just doing this could be a very time-consuming and complex effort.

After this, the employer needed to obtain labor certification from the Department of Labor, and for that, the employer had to give proof that the beneficiary would receive the prevailing wage, and that domestic employees were notified of the imminent hire of a foreigner. The Department of Labor reviewed the evidence and then issued the labor certification, a process that often took at least a month or longer. After all this, the employer filed the formal petition itself, which typically involved a form (I-129), but because it took so much trouble to get to this point in the first place, employers routinely included a narrative about themselves and the beneficiaries they wish to hire. Sometimes, employers attached exhibits and other documentary evidence about their company or industry, as well as laudatory information about their beneficiaries, including copies of their degrees and university transcripts. In the end, it was rather common for firms to spend a lot of money and time hiring an H-1B worker; for many, the process involved the assistance of lawyers who specialized in employment-related migration.[14]

The Immigration Act of 1990 also created several new visas that had previously fallen within the H-1. The O was a non-immigrant visa for persons of "extraordinary ability," typically meant for entertainers, athletes, and internationally recognized scholars, business people, scientists, and artists. There was, and still is, no cap on the O, since presumably such exceptional people wouldn't be harmful to anyone.[15] In recent years, the majority of persons entering under the O were from Europe, with Asia a distant second.[16] Next, the P visa was also meant for athletes and entertainers, but not necessarily ones who were "extraordinary." Under the P, they had to be at least "internationally recognized," and no more than 25,000 could enter in any given fiscal year.[17] Finally, two other visas, the R for religious workers, and the Q for persons in international cultural exchange programs, were created under the Act of 1990. Both were described only briefly, and neither generated any meaningful debate. But the O and P visas were especially important, because in the period immediately prior to 1990, the majority of persons receiving an H-1 were entertainers and athletes, not engineers or nurses.[18]

A Shortage of Workers

When the H-1 was re-phrased in the Act of 1990, several influential scholars of immigration law wondered whether the annual cap of 65,000 persons would ever be reached, especially in light of older trends, and also because of the new bureaucratic hurdles facing employers of H-1B non-immigrants.[19] But in fiscal year 1997, the INS reported that the cap had actually been reached for the first time ever, about five weeks before September 30, 1997. H-1Bs granted after the cap was reached were charged against the quota for the following year, so in the following year, the visas ran out in May. The new set of petitioners for the H-1B were high-technology companies—firms in the burgeoning information technology, or "IT," industry—firms that within the past ten years were growing incredibly powerful and rich. By the mid-1990s, over half of all H-1B beneficiaries were working for IT firms, and their collective discovery of this temporary visa made it increasingly visible. By the late 1990s, corporate demand for these visas was obviously exceeding supply.[20]

After one of the most sharp and contentious policy debates over immigration in recent years, President Bill Clinton signed into law the American Competitiveness and Workforce Improvement Act (ACWIA) of 1998, in October of that year.[21] This new law immediately increased the number of H-1B visas: "115,000 in fiscal year 1999, 115,000 in fiscal year 2000, 107,500 in fiscal year 2001," and then back to "65,000 in each succeeding fiscal year."[22] The law had had several influential sponsors in Congress, including Republican Senators Spencer Abraham and Orrin Hatch, the powerful Chairman of the Senate Judiciary Committee. In congressional hearings in February and April of 1998, Senator Hatch set the tone for the new bill removing the cap on the H-1B:

> It is estimated that about ten percent of this country's current information technology jobs are vacant and that this critical shortage of programmers, systems analysts, and computer engineers will increase significantly in the next decade. According to the Department of Commerce, the United States will generate more than 100,000 information technology jobs each year for the next decade. Notably, the vast majority of high-tech firms cite the shortage of skilled workers as the leading barrier to their company's growth and competitiveness in the global marketplace.

For Senator Hatch, an increase in the number of skilled workers was not just a sound national policy, it was good local politics: "In few places is this shortage more acute than in my own state of Utah where the high tech industry grew by 12 percent in 1996 and where our 1,900 high tech companies plan to add almost 20,000 jobs annually in the next three years. The primary potential impediment to our state's growth is the shortage of skilled workers."[23]

Several influential companies sent representatives to elaborate on the details of this purported shortage of workers: persons testifying to the Senate Committee included vice presidents from Sun Microsystems, Microsoft, and Cypress Semiconductors, as well as the Dean of the College of Engineering from the University of Michigan.[24] Outside Congress, several other major companies and institutions also spoke of the shortage of skilled workers in various IT fields.[25]

The major corporations trying to increase the cap for H-1Bs all complained of a critical shortage of highly trained workers for IT firms in an industry that they characterized as increasingly global and competitive. They warned that if highly trained workers were not welcomed in greater numbers into the United States, other countries with burgeoning high-technology industries would gain competitive advantages. Kenneth Alvarez of Sun Microsystems provided testimony to the Senate that was typical of this position:

> [There is a] shortage of qualified workers to fill crucial positions in the information technology sector. This deficit of skilled workers, if not remedied quickly, will result in lost business opportunities, slower innovation, and diminished productivity overall. Those developments would seriously hinder our ability to compete, and the high-tech industry's ability to continue the sort of rapid creation of jobs this country has benefited from.

Restricting the admission of the highly skilled would threaten the economy of the United States: "Ultimately, a prolonged worker shortage could cause U.S. high tech companies to lose their dominant position in the world market."[26]

This theme was reiterated often, whether by the president of single prominent firms ("The high-tech sector is growing exponentially, causing chronic shortages") or by the president of the Information Technology Association of America, which is perhaps the most influential trade organization representing several different kinds of IT firms, including AT&T, Dell, Hewlett-Packard, IBM, Intel, Lockheed, Oracle, and Yahoo. "Access to the IT industry's basic commodity—skilled people—has reached a perilous state," according to one executive.[27] The essence of this argument was that a restriction on the migration of the highly skilled—the most indispensable resource in this industry—would exacerbate labor shortages for important domestic firms in a critical area of the economy.

Several leaders of IT firms spoke very highly of the current benefits of the H-1B program, and of the non-immigrants they had employed in a wide range of positions. For some, these workers were "a critical element of our success," and without them, key products would not have proceeded into the market.[28] Moreover, under this theory, these workers created jobs for other workers, having a kind of multiplier effect on the labor market for domestic workers. The CEO of Cypress Semiconductors explained this phenomenon thus: "Cypress has 470 engineers and 2,771 worldwide employees. Roughly speaking, this means each engineer creates jobs for six additional people who make or administrate or sell the products developed by our engineers. A disproportionate number of our R&D engineers—about 36.6%—are staffed by immigrants, a typical situation at high-tech companies. It follows that if we had been prevented from hiring the 172 immigrant researchers we have hired, we would have failed to create about 1,000 other jobs—70% of which are held by native-born Americans. Immigrant engineers not only do not take away jobs, they actually create jobs for native-born Americans."[29] Again, this argument was repeated several times in congressional testimony, and in news sources covering the passage of the Act of 1998.[30] Altogether, the idea was that rather than *taking* jobs from American citizens, these persons *increased* the opportunities available to American citizens, mostly by creating new economic activity and new jobs that would otherwise not exist.

In addition, in a global marketplace, IT products had to be "localized," such that software or hardware originally produced for an American market could be altered significantly for consumers based in Asia, Europe, or other parts of the world. Software had to be rewritten to account for differences in language, for example, before it could be marketed abroad. Non-immigrants were in a unique position to "localize" products made by American companies, thereby securing higher profits for those companies in the form of increased overseas sales.[31] In a global marketplace, one needs a flexible global workforce. And if skilled persons couldn't come to take jobs here, American firms might be forced to take these jobs abroad. These types of comments were often presented as ominous warnings sprinkled throughout congressional testimony: "We may even be forced to move production to locations overseas to make sure we can find the workers we need."[32]

Perhaps because the shortage of labor was so acute, their talents so necessary, several companies proposed even more radical changes to American immigration law. For example, Michael Murray, an officer at Microsoft, recommended that a greater fraction of highly skilled workers should be allowed to settle as permanent residents: he noted that the current immigration quotas passed in 1990 effectively limited individual sending countries to no more than 9,800 employment-based permanent residency visas per year:

> [But] because certain Asian Pacific nations produce a large number of highly qualified, highly skilled individuals, the visa backlogs for an individual from these countries is significant, resulting in processing delays of up to four years. Unless the per-country limit is adjusted, many of these individuals will be forced to go abroad when their H-1B visas expire. This will result not only in significant disruptions to their U.S. employers, but may enhance the competitive prospects of several foreign countries, such as Germany and Japan, whose software industries have recently become significant competitors.[33]

In other words, if skilled workers were forced to resettle from the United States after their six-year H-1B had expired, they would be excellent candidates for migration into another country that competed with the United States. Again, as others had suggested, unless these workers could find a permanent home here, they could give other countries economic and technological advantages.

If anything, the congressional testimony over the H-1B showed that at the very least, an impressive group of corporations had come to rely on this visa. These firms were not located in some margin of the mainstream economy—they *were* the mainstream economy. IT firms had generated billions of dollars in sales, and firms like Microsoft, Oracle, and Dell were projected to become even stronger and more economically vital than in the two previous decades when they had come into existence. These companies competed fiercely with one another—the ferociousness with which they competed provided the material for books, magazines, PBS specials, and even a few feature-length movies. In fiction and in real life, many of the founders and leaders of these firms were well known public figures, even though they occasionally feuded publicly.[34]

Yet they achieved a remarkable degree of consensus over the need to hire foreign workers in this critical industry, even if they had to pay a premium to get them. In the spring and summer of 1998, powerful American politicians were inclined to give them what they wanted, as pro-business Republicans like John McCain, Phil Gramm, and Orrin Hatch came to an understanding with pro-growth Democrats like Charles Robb and President Bill Clinton. Ideologically, these politicians occasionally loathed one another, too, but on this issue, they achieved a remarkable consensus.

PROTECTING AMERICAN WORKERS: LOSING THE DISTINCTION BETWEEN IMMIGRANT AND NON-IMMIGRANT

The H-1B did have its staunch opponents, and before Congress, in that first set of critical hearings, major think-tanks, professional associations, and some academics spoke against the H-1B in general, as well as any increase in the annual cap. Almost all of their testimony critiqued the purported shortage of workers in high-technology industries, as well as alleged abuse of the program overall. For example, a researcher for the Urban Institute noted that "despite the extravagant claims of a shortage of IT workers, the indicators are mixed." In certain sectors, there was a decrease in the demand for labor: "Employment in operations research has actually declined since 1988 and the total number of computer programmers remained at about 560,000 workers between 1988 and 1996, a time in which employment of all professionals expanded by nearly 30 percent."[35]

The president of the Institute of Electrical and Electronics Engineers, USA, one of the leading professional associations for highly skilled professionals in a wide range of technical fields, also insisted that there was no shortage, and that instead, powerful IT firms were using the H-1B for less than admirable purposes.[36] John Reinert said that "[H-1B] has been widely used by many employers to provide a probationary try-out employment program for illegal (out of status) aliens, foreign students and foreign visitors to determine if they should be sponsored for permanent resident status." Foreign workers under the H-1B were beholden to their corporate sponsors, and not likely to complain about substandard wages and working conditions.

Critics suggested that for many firms, these workers were attractive precisely because they were cheaper and more exploitable, charges that may in fact be true.[37] They also claimed the IT industry used foreign workers to depress wages for domestic workers, the H-1B related thus to the H-2A, the H-1B spawning a new and depressing industry for high tech "braceros."[38] Altogether, the critics implied that selfish American corporations were undermining American workers by importing cheap foreign labor.

Most interesting of these critics was Norman Matloff, a professor of computer science at the University of California at Davis. For several months, Professor Matloff maintained an interactive website that collected newspaper accounts, scholarly articles, and the testimony of people in the IT industry, all to show that the major firms in the industry were essentially lying about the shortage of qualified workers. "There is no such shortage," Matloff said. Rather, "Age discrimination is rampant in the industry." IT firms were opting to hire cheap foreign labor and newly minted college graduates (also relatively cheap labor), rather than retaining older workers or reinvesting in training programs to keep current workers up to date. Moreover, the H-1B was effectively becoming a back door toward permanent settlement in the United States: "Though industry lobbyists dismiss the H-1B workers as comprising only a small fraction of their workforces, this is highly misleading, as it does not count the workers who first began work in the U.S. under the H-1B program but then were sponsored by the employers for permanent residence. About 35% of Silicon Valley programmers and engineers are foreign born, and most were originally hired via the H-1B program."[39]

The line between temporary and permanent migrants was indeed blurry. According to data analyzed by the Immigration Service, persons under the H-1B had a rather high likelihood of adjusting into permanent residency—they had petitioned for "adjustments of status" at a rate hovering around 50% for persons admitted since 1995. The net result was the same: by introducing so many foreign workers, American companies could cast aside older, more highly paid engineers in favor of cheaper foreign labor.[40] In effect, immigration rules were "deleting American workers."[41]

These arguments weighed heavily in both chambers of Congress. Legislators sympathetic to charges of H-1B abuse, or to claims of harm to domestic workers, almost derailed the passage of the Act of 1998. Senator Tom Harkin of Iowa delayed the final vote in the Senate, and influential leaders in the House—including Lamar Smith—expressed deep reservations about any increase in the cap. Tom Harkin, a close political ally of Richard Gephardt, represented protectionist interests in the Senate; Lamar Smith was, among many things, not particularly sympathetic to immigrants during his tenure in the House, although his voting record was obviously pro-business.[42]

Efforts to achieve a compromise with these legislators proved successful after leaders proposed substantial changes to the H-1B program. The Act of 1998 increased the H-1B cap for three consecutive fiscal years, but it was full of new regulations and definitions, higher fees, and long-range plans to remedy whatever labor shortages may (or may not) exist in high-technology industries. In the last portions of the Act, Congress commissioned several studies to examine further just how serious the purported labor shortages were, and whether age discrimination or lower and depressed wages were as common as critics had complained.[43]

First, in addition to raising the cap on H-1B visas in fiscal years 1999, 2000, and 2001, the Act of 1998 increased fees for all petitioners. All firms requesting an H-1B had to submit a $110 filing fee per petition; the new rule required an additional $500 per petition on top of the filing fee. Under §414 of the Act, this money was put into an "H-1B Non-Immigrant Petitioner Account," then divvied up into programs ranging from scholarships to "low-income students enrolled in a program of study leading to a degree in mathematics, engineering, or computer science," "programs that provide opportunities for enrollment in year-round academic enrichment courses in mathematics, engineering, or science" run by the National Science Foundation, and "demonstration programs or projects to provide technical skills training for workers, including both employed and unemployed workers."[44] This combination of academic scholarships and job training would presumably work to eliminate the need for foreign workers. Since wealthy corporations would pay the $500 per non-immigrant, it was as though the Act embodied a redistributive principle—taking fees from wealthy corporations and then distributing them to low-income students. Based on the new number of H-1B visas that would be authorized, as well as the backlog from fiscal year 1998, the rule would yield a substantial sum, at least $75 million just in the first year.

The Act also provided for several new provisions intended to protect American workers, but which also improved working conditions for non-immigrant workers in the process. For example, as a strictly protectionist measure, one provision distinguished firms that happened to hire H-1B workers versus firms that had become "H-1B dependent." Firms that were "H-1B dependent" were treated differently: they couldn't lay off any American workers 90 days before or after hiring a foreign one, and they had to file papers confirming that they had taken all good-faith measures to recruit American workers. Congress also noted that some IT firms act as recruitment, placement, or consulting firms—they gathered a range of workers, often from abroad, then contracted their workers' services as consultants to other established firms. Pejoratively, these firms were referred to as "body shops," and they were precisely the type of "H-1B-dependent" companies that worried legislators had had in mind. These companies could not place workers in other firms if those other firms had laid off a similar worker 90 days before or after the placement of an H-1B worker. If any of these rules were breached, yet another provision provided whistle-blower protections for any worker reporting the breach to the Department of Labor. Firms found in violation of these provisions would be heavily fined, up to $5,000, and then forbidden from petitioning for another H-1B for at least two years.[45] The overriding goal of all of these new provisions was to protect domestic workers, and that goal was approached in such a way as to eventually eliminate the need for foreign labor.

Other aspects of the law had significant consequences in pursuit of this same objective. Indeed, the Act of 1998 *reduced* the disparities in bargaining position between foreign and domestic workers, such that firms were more likely to treat foreign and domestic workers as rough equivalents. For example, under one provision, firms hiring non-immigrant H-1B workers had to furnish them with the same fringe benefits as any domestic worker in an equivalent position. Foreign workers had to have the same or equivalent life and health insurance, retirement and savings plans, opportunities for bonuses, even stock options. Non-immigrant workers could not be "benched," meaning that they could not be left unemployed during the period for which the visa was granted, nor could they be assigned a different job at a lower wage. Petitioning employers had to pay the wage they had specified in the original immigration petition. That wage, of course, had to be the prevailing wage for all persons in that type of job; anything lower would trigger investigations, fines, and other unpleasant consequences.

Although these measures were intended to protect American workers, they also diminished the distinction between "American" and "foreign," as well as the distinction between "immigrant" and "non-immigrant." For firms that were regarded as "H-1B-dependent," the set of rules for H-1B non-immigrants were very analogous to the complex labor certification process for visas under the second or third preferences for employment-based immigrants. In the desire to protect American citizens from the foreigners, Congress had implemented rules that made citizens and foreigners more alike under the law, in terms of wages, benefits, hiring, and other working conditions.[46] The one crucial distinction was that American workers did not have to worry about having to leave the United States should they ever lose their jobs. By 2000, persons who did have these non-immigrant visas—those who would have exactly these kinds of worries—were much more likely to be from Asia than anywhere else.

CHAPTER 7

Engineering the Model Minority

A Global Competition for Talented Individuals

The debate over the H-1B did not diminish after the passage of the Act of 1998. This was because in June of 1999, three months before the end of the 1999 fiscal year, the Immigration Service once again ran out of H-1B visas. New applicants would have to wait, and those who were considered after the 115,000 cap had been reached would be charged in the coming fiscal year. In fiscal year 2000, the visas would run out in March. Various parties—including corporate lobbying groups, think tanks, economists for the Federal Reserve, and leading politicians—began contemplating yet another increase in the ceiling in the spring of 1999. Senator Orrin Hatch commissioned a report that detailed the debate within the Senate Judiciary Committee about an increase in the cap, under a new rule entitled the American Competitiveness in the Twenty-First Century Act (AC21). The Committee supported the rule under Hatch's direction, in large part by phrasing it as though it were within the nation's economic interests. The Report heavily cited the remarks of advocates for highly skilled labor who argued that "a global competition for talented individuals is indeed taking place."[1]

Debate over the new rules had also changed, chiefly because a small but vocal group of H-1B recipients were themselves involved in the shaping of AC21. Led by organizations like the Immigrants Support Network, whose leaders were largely South Asian H-1B recipients working in IT firms, these participants were situated in an unusual place: though they were clearly not American citizens, they actively lobbied Congress to make the terms of the H-1B more humane, as well as providing labor protections and safeguards similar to the ones enjoyed by their American peers. Many were obviously prospective Americans—they complained, for example, that even when they petitioned for permanent residency, as they were allowed to do under the Act of 1990, backlogs at the INS meant that their petitions were still being adjudicated when their H-1B status expired.[2] This left them in a legal limbo, forced to leave even as they were requesting permission to stay permanently. Others felt trapped and underappreciated at their firms, required to work in unpleasant conditions just to maintain lawful immigration status.

By 2000, the Immigrants Support Network counted 12,000 active members, and it had hired leading attorneys and lobbying firms to make its case before Congress.[3] In contrast, although major labor unions like the AFL-CIO were formally opposed to an expansion of the H-1B program, their opposition was tempered, and many of their leaders seemed to acknowledge that an increase was inevitable. Indeed, over the past twenty years, major labor unions like the International Ladies' Garment Workers' Union (ILGWU) and the Service Employees International Union (SEIU) had taken pro-immigrant positions, but no major labor union had yet organized highly skilled H-1B workers.[4] Organizations like the Immigrant Support Network were developing significant lobbying efforts, and thus performing a traditional function of labor unions.

Table 7.1 and Table 7.2 show profiles of H-1B workers admitted to the United States in fiscal year 2001. From Table 7.1, one can see that the fraction of beneficiaries from India was striking: close to half of all H-1B recipients were South Asian Indian. South Asian Indian H-1B beneficiaries have always constituted the majority of H-1B recipients in recent years, and certainly since the Competitiveness Act of 1998. In its analysis of the H-1B, the Immigration Service said: "The typical H-1B beneficiary whose petition was approved in fiscal year 2001 had the following characteristics: born in India; 29 years old; holding a bachelor's degree; working in a computer-related occupation; and receiving an annual compensation of $55,000. Forty-one percent of all beneficiaries were born in India, had either a bachelor's or master's degree, and were employed in a computer-related occupation."[5]

Table 7.2 shows that almost all H-1B beneficiaries were highly skilled workers in science and technology fields, and that a majority worked primarily in computer-related occupations, including software development, system design, and technology consulting. The figure for fiscal year 2001 for this first category, however, reflects an overall decline since 1999, when

TABLE 7.1 Profile of H-1B Beneficiaries by Leading Countries of Birth (2001)

	All Beneficiaries	Percent
All	331,206	100.00%
India	161,561	48.78%
P.R. China	27,331	8.25%
Canada	12,726	3.84%
Philippines	10,389	3.14%
United Kingdom	9,682	2.92%
Korea	6,468	1.95%
Pakistan	6,313	1.91%
Japan	5,902	1.78%
Taiwan	5,808	1.75%
Russia	4,589	1.39%
All Asian countries	245,442	74.11%
Mexico	3,987	1.20%
Central America	943	0.28%

Source: Immigration and Naturalization Service, *2001 Statistical Yearbook* 135, 192, 195 (2002)

TABLE 7.2 Profile of H-1B Beneficiaries by Occupation (2001)

	Total	Percent
All	331,206	100.00%
Computer-related	191,397	57.79%
Architecture, engineering, and survey	40,388	12.19%
Administrative specialization	23,794	7.18%
Education	17,431	5.26%
Managers and officials n.e.c.	12,423	3.75%
Medicine and health	11,334	3.42%
Life sciences	6,492	1.96%
Social sciences	6,145	1.86%
Mathematical and physical sciences	5,772	1.74%
Misc. professional, technical, and managerial	5,662	1.71%

Source: Immigration and Naturalization Service, *2001 Statistical Yearbook* 136 (2002)

this category accounted for 61.6 percent of all beneficiaries. Other occupations, including architecture, engineering and survey, administrative specialization, and managers and officials, held a greater share of beneficiaries, signaling the occupational diversification of H-1B visa workers. In addition, university sponsorship of H-1B programs since 1998 has led to greater use of this visa in academic research settings; the fact that more beneficiaries are working in education, as well as in the life sciences, the social sciences, and mathematical and physical sciences also reflects diversification.

Still, the beneficiaries in the aggregate had much in common. They were relatively young, highly educated, generally well paid compared with the majority of workers, and very likely to work in major IT firms, academic research centers, or in other technology sectors. In fact, as group, these migrants were some of the best-educated, highly trained migrants in American immigration history. Since 1998, over two thirds of all H-1B beneficiaries were from Asia, a portion that has only increased in recent years. When these educated, technologically literate groups of "non-immigrants" began lobbying for changes in law favorable to their condition, they were received with a substantial degree of political support from leading companies, and from sympathetic pro-business political leaders.

Indeed, with the support of leading pro-business Republicans, Senator Orrin Hatch proposed yet another new ceiling for the H-1B. Most of the Democratic members of the Judiciary Committee would vote in favor of this increase, but in early legislative discussions, they inserted a minority opinion in the Senate Report issued in support of Hatch's proposal. They conceded that "unless we take steps now to address this growing workforce gap, American's technological and economic leadership will be jeopardized." But with reference to the cap, "this increase must be temporary, reasonable, and sufficiently tailored to meet existing short-term needs." Above all, it should protect the interests and long-term prospects of American workers. Toward that end, Senator Edward Kennedy had recommended an increase to 145,000 per fiscal year, plus an additional 10,000 to 14,000 H-1Bs for anyone with a master's degree or higher; Senator Hatch had proposed an increase to 195,000, and any H-1B beneficiary in an institution of higher education, in any organization affiliated with such an institution, or any nonprofit or governmental research institution would be completely exempt from the cap.

In practice, Hatch's proposal could yield as many as a quarter million new H-1B visas per year. Leading Democrats—Patrick Leahy, Edward Kennedy, Joseph Biden, Russell Feingold, Robert Torricelli, and Charles Schumer—finally agreed to this very reluctantly, and hinged their support for Hatch's proposal on a new set of provisions to protect and increase the supply of domestic workers in information technology. They said again that, "A modest increase in the H-1B high-tech visa cap is justified. But this increase must be temporary, reasonable, and sufficiently tailored to meet existing short-term needs." The Senators were also concerned about fraud, and recommended measures to discover the extent of the problem.[6]

So much was uncertain, and many legislators felt that this was one issue where they really did have to navigate a sea of uncertainty. For example, in a study sent to Congress, Stuart Anderson, an analyst at the Cato Institute, insisted that fraud was not rampant among H-1B petitioners: relying on statistics and controversial cases investigated by the Department of Labor, Anderson concluded that "there has been a lot of smoke, but little fire relating to alleged abuses."[7] And yet so many media accounts revolved solely around instances of fraud.[8] Government agencies were inconclusive: in a report released one month before the Act became law, the General Accounting Office said that although the system for procuring H-1B visas was inefficient and prone to abuse, there was no conclusive evidence that fraud and misrepresentation were "rampant." Moreover, it was obvious in the report that the GAO and the INS could not agree about the extent of the problems in processing and granting H-1B petitions, with the former suggesting that more needed to be done, and the INS insisting that the current system was sufficient to catch fraud and noncompliance.[9]

There was also substantial disagreement on other important issues. For instance, many opponents of the H-1B kept insisting that this was yet another back door into the United States, much like refugee policy under the Act of 1980, or the mass legalizations authorized by the Act of 1986. Yet, the most recent scholarship did suggest that although highly skilled workers were, in fact, being sought after in a number of different countries, they were much more likely to travel widely and perhaps "settle" nowhere. In her study of medical professionals and science and technical workers, for instance, Robin Iredale noted that several nations—Australia, Canada, and the United Kingdom—had altered immigration rules to attract highly skilled professionals. But, she concluded, as all of these nations, including the United States, competed for these same workers, these workers were increasingly flexible in terms of location. Many worked for firms that were truly international. Thus, "as international labor markets become predominant, the drive for labor self-sufficiency may no longer be appropriate or necessary."[10] Other leading scholars tended to confirm this phenomenon: "Research suggests that 'brain drain' may be giving way to a process of 'brain circulation,' as talented immigrants who study and work in the United States return to their home countries to take advantage of promising opportunities there." Thus, "it is no longer valid to assume that skilled immigrants will stay permanently in the United States," or any other country for that matter.[11]

These scholars suggested that rather than a back door, the flexibility and temporary nature of the H-1B was part of a new revolving door for the highly skilled. Instead of choosing to settle permanently in the United States, as some had suggested, the new classes of professional migrants might just take whatever expertise and experience might be had here, then look for opportunities elsewhere. Above all, "place" was becoming less important.[12]

QUESTIONING THE SHORTAGE

In a flurry of testimony in the House Subcommittee on Immigration in August of 2000, just before the passage of AC21, organized labor groups and professional associations again protested another doubling of H-1B visas. The president of the Institute of Electrical and Electronics Engineers called any increase in the cap "premature": "In the absence of reliable statistics to support industry's contention that there is a serious national shortage of core information technology workers, including engineers and scientists, systems analysts and programmers, there is insufficient empirical evidence to justify another increase in H-1B admissions ceilings at this time."[13]

David Smith, the director of policy of the AFL-CIO, echoed these concerns: "What we do not know is that there is no substantial proof of a widespread worker shortage as claimed by the information technology industry." Smith cited high unemployment rates among older programmers, and what seemed to be a growing, "voracious" appetite for foreign workers in the IT industry. He advocated long-term projects to address whatever shortages might or might not exist. Current policies were unacceptable: "The H-1B program and its expansion have proven to be the worst possible scenario for U.S. workers."[14]

The leading Republican on the House Subcommittee, Lamar Smith, heard these objections sympathetically, but he seemed to concede:

> Although there is still no objective, credible study that documents a shortage of American high-tech workers, the INS said recently that the demand for highly skilled foreign workers is running at least 50,000 ahead of last year. Such a demand can indicate an actual shortage of American workers, a spot shortage, a preference for cheap labor or replacement workers, or something else. But because

of the importance of the high-tech industry to our economy, I think we should give the industry the benefit of the doubt.[15]

This "benefit of the doubt" meant going along with Orrin Hatch's proposal toward an unprecedented rise in the H-1B cap. If all of these visas were used, then more persons would enter under this one category than all permanent residents seeking employment visas in all industries. This was an astounding shift in the law governing employment-based migration.

Under the American Competitiveness in the Twenty-First Century Act of 2000, passed in October of 2000, the H-1B cap was raised yet again: "195,000 in fiscal year 2001; 195,000 in fiscal year 2002; and 195,000 in fiscal year 2003." In addition, the Act of 2000 provided additional visas for fiscal years 1999 and 2000, so that they would not obstruct the cap for fiscal year 2001. Along the lines of Hatch's original proposal, the Act of 2000 provided that persons working in "institutions of higher education or a related or affiliated nonprofit entity" or for "a nonprofit research organization or a governmental research organization," *and* persons with advanced degrees wouldn't be counted against the cap.[16] Various redistributive provisions were strengthened: "measures were adopted to encourage more U.S. students to study mathematics, engineering, and computer science and to train more U.S. workers in these areas." Monies taken from fees collected for H-1B beneficiaries would "result in total funding of $450,000,000, which would allow for 40,000 scholarships to be awarded to U.S. students."[17]

Also, the position of non-immigrant H-1B beneficiaries improved substantially: Congress made the H-1B more "portable," saying that the beneficiaries were "authorized to accept new employment upon the filing by the prospective employer of a new petition on behalf of such non-immigrant." In other words, if they found a better job, they could take it, provided that their new employer filed another H-1B petition with the proper immigration authorities.[18] Moreover, if H-1B non-immigrants had filed a petition for permanent residency—thus attempting to adjust their status to that of immigrants—they could request an extension of their non-immigrant status in "one-year increments until such time as a final decision is made on the alien's lawful permanent residence" petition.[19] In practice, non-immigrants under an H-1B who wished to remain in the United States after the six-year period could simply file a petition for permanent residency, and so long as the final petition was winding its way through the immigration bureaucracy for at least a year, they could work and remain in the United States indefinitely.

Most importantly, the Act of 2000 waived the per country limit on employment-based visas, just as Michael Murray, the vice president of

Microsoft, had suggested in his testimony to the Senate in February of 1998. Countries that were heavily impacted for employment-based visas—especially India—could see substantial numbers adjusting into permanent residency. The greater ease with which H-1B beneficiaries could seek permanent residency greatly empowered these beneficiaries in the labor market, and gave them much more leverage in the ultimate decision of whether to leave or to remain in the United States. All of these changes amounted to a major victory for groups like the Immigrant Support Network.

THE ENGINEERING OF A MODEL MINORITY

In this way, the obscure H-1 visa—once reserved for athletes, entertainers, and fashion models—had evolved into an entirely different thing. Vast changes in the American economy and society now provided a wide new avenue for large numbers of highly skilled professionals entering the United States, and it was obvious that many were intending to stay permanently. There is no historical analog for the H-1B program—nowhere in American immigration history has Congress provided for such tremendous numbers of highly paid, highly skilled immigrant workers. The cap for H-1B immigrants in 2001 far exceeded the cap for immigrant-based employment visas, the first time that a non-immigrant category for employment exceeded the cap for an immigrant category. The method and proof required to secure entry were roughly the same—the distinction in law between a temporary worker and a permanent worker had almost disappeared. The sheer scale of the new migration was impressive: in fiscal year 2000, 137,000 H-1B visas for initial employment in American firms were approved; in the following fiscal year, 201,000 H-1B visas were approved. From October 2000 to June 2001, 254,000 new H-1B visa petitions were approved. The last time so many immigrant workers came so suddenly was at the height of the Bracero Program, when about 445,000 Mexican workers were brought to work as agricultural laborers.[20]

Most striking of all was how the legislative debates about the H-1B *avoided* issues of race. That is, proponents of a higher ceiling and opponents of temporary-worker programs occasionally made references to "Asian" workers, and the opponents often said that these workers were driving down the wages and working conditions of "native" workers; thematically, much of what they said resembled the protests of white labor unions that had complained about the arrival of Chinese laborers in the 19th century. Certainly, in media accounts of the debate, various participants—journalists, workers in the IT industry, and members of the public—did say race-conscious and racially hostile things about H-1B workers. But in formal proceedings, in testimony to Congress, and even in public, the most visible opponents of the H-1B attempted to insulate themselves *against* charges of racial bias. Professor Norman Matloff insisted that he was not, for example, anti-Asian, because his own wife was in fact a Chinese immigrant, and because his professional work in computer science included the development of software technology in Asia.[21] None of the Congressional testimony included pejorative or racist claims about H-1B workers, nor accused the central participants in the debate of blatant racial bias.

During the late 19th century, Chinese immigrants were referred to as an "Oriental gangrene," and in the early 20th, Japanese immigrants were described as a "yellow peril." American politicians and judges had uttered these slurs, often while campaigning for office or deciding significant legal disputes. Working together, they created the entire substance of immigration law in the United States to keep these immigrants out. A hundred or even fifty years ago, if 140,000 "temporary" Asian workers were arriving alongside another 100,000 permanent workers from Asia into the United States every year, then they might have concluded that "[this] immigration was in numbers approaching the character of an invasion, and was a menace to our civilization."[22]

Yet instead of race or racial disaster, the ongoing debates about the H-1B in particular and about employment-based migration in general focused almost entirely on economic costs and benefits, about efficiencies in a global market, and about the competitive advantages needed to sustain the United States. The racial profile of H-1B workers was not as open a public issue—the more compelling concern was whether their entry would harm American workers, or whether powerful companies could survive without them. Legislators assured concerned union leaders that they could stop the flow of H-1B workers rather easily, even as they also assured the leaders of prominent technology firms that they would provide whatever level of non-immigrant labor was necessary. Again, the debate was not so much about culture, or about who could or could not pass into American citizenship racially; it was conducted in the language of the market, so as to frame immigration law in a way that would promote efficiency and maximize benefits to American economy and society. As in discussions about deportation, welfare, refugees, and family reunification, the themes of market efficiency would come to dominate immigration policy in the United States.

In terms of numbers, the overall effect of the new immigration policy will have clear, racial consequences, especially for Asians. More immigrants from Asia are likely to arrive for employment than ever before.

If one includes "temporary" skilled workers from Asia, that trend will be reinforced. In fact, one *must* include "temporary" workers from this measure because so many of them have become "permanent." In 1985, about 8,000 persons on H visas adjusted to permanent-resident status. That figure climbed to 10,000 by 1988, and 14,600 by 1990. Rates have been high since then—34,700 in 1992 and 39,000 in 1993. In 2001, more than 85,000 persons adjusted to permanent resident status from various non-immigrant temporary visa categories. About three quarters of all people who adjusted status in this way—62,300 persons—were from Asia.[23] As we mentioned toward the end of Chapter 5, in 2001, of the 179,000 immigrants who came under employment-based visas, 106,000 were from Asia.[24] In conjunction with the deportation rules that quickly remove even former refugees, and family reunification rules that disqualify or discourage the reunion of family members in the United States, these trends are likely to enhance the notion that Asian Americans nationally are a "model minority." Immigration law—the sum of the new methods of exclusion, inclusion, and removal—makes this possibility much more likely than ever before.

CHAPTER 8

Probationary Americans

"Come Out of Hiding"

On January 17, 2004, President George Bush proposed a new temporary worker program targeted at poorer immigrant workers from Mexico, one that probably would have been introduced earlier in his administration but for the attacks on September 11th. Flanked by his own cabinet, the Mexican Ambassador Tony Garza, and a host of Mexican American and Latino civil rights leaders, President Bush called for "a new temporary worker program that will match willing foreign workers with willing American employers, when no American can be found to fill the jobs." He also stressed that "foreign workers" would include "undocumented immigrants," who could join temporary worker programs so that they could "come out of hiding and participate legally in America's economy."[1]

The following day, Bush's proposal for a temporary worker program and the suggestion for a new path for legalized status for undocumented immigrants were both met with a flurry of negative reactions. Former Republican Presidential candidate Patrick Buchanan criticized the President for granting a "blanket amnesty for 8 to 10 million illegal aliens," and then he wondered, in light of so many millions of unemployed Americans, "What in heaven's name is the President of the United States doing inviting foreign workers to come into the United States to take jobs?" While Buchanan saw the temporary worker program solely as a threat to American workers, John Sweeney, the president of AFL-CIO, criticized the program's "potential for abuse and exploitation" of temporary workers and cautioned that the program would "create a permanent underclass of workers who are unable to fully participate in democracy." Some labeled the proposals as "Bush's Bracero Program," and said that the President's motives were political in nature—to win more Latino votes, and to gain Mexico's support for American foreign policy—and not driven by a concern for people who were actually "in hiding."[2]

By 2004, not only were there many more undocumented aliens in the United States than in 1996, the immigration law had evolved over that time in a way likely to discourage undocumented aliens from "participating" in the United States at all. It was an odd thing for the President to suggest that undocumented immigrants—persons most likely to be deported summarily upon detection—should "come out." Many feared that this was an underhanded plan for federal officials to identify more and more people who had entered illegally, so that in the near or even distant future, such officials could expeditiously "remove" them. A provision in the plan itself indicated that once the temporary "guest worker" visa had expired, the immigrant beneficiary was required to return back to his native country.[3] From the perspective of many immigrants, this did not sound like the President was inviting workers from Mexico or anywhere else to participate *permanently* in American society.

EFFICIENCY AND FLEXIBILITY

The President's latest immigration proposals underscored the profound differences in perspective between the lawmakers governing immigration and the immigrants governed by American law. From the federal government's point of view, a guest worker program for poorer Mexican and Latino immigrants had the primary advantage of increasing contacts between state agencies and immigrants, who could then be better monitored and tracked once in the United States. It was likely to please larger agricultural growers in the Southwest, major slaughterhouses in the Midwest and South, and garment industry subcontractors in Southern California, as these were the types of firms that had employed large numbers of undocumented aliens in recent years.[4] Legalizing the flow of these workers might thus increase surveillance of, and efficiencies in, several areas of the economy that had already become dependent on poor laborers from Mexico, Central America, and Asia.

From the perspective of the immigrants, however, the law had become so harsh that it was much more rational to avoid it. They had little to gain: even if they were "legalized," federal officials could still invoke the various provisions of the Anti-Terrorism Act, the Welfare Act, or the Responsibility Act to forbid them from relying on any form of public assistance, or to remove them for becoming a public charge, or to remove them for a single criminal conviction. No one could deny the ease and speed with which public officials could now remove persons permanently from the United States, nor could anyone deny that American welfare law has left immigrants to fend for themselves. In addition, because most poorer immigrant laborers would earn a low wage, and because of the deeming provisions and the new affidavits of support and the threshold income requirements, family reunification would probably not be an option for the majority of poorer workers. Most will easily figure out that family reunification as a principle no longer applies to those who are poor. Therefore, coming into contact with the law provided relatively few benefits, but it could generate a substantial amount of anxiety for tens of thousands of migrants.

The very flexibility of contemporary employment-based immigration law was another source of anxiety for immigrants, even while government officials might see this flexibility as a key improvement in controlling migratory flows. In the months leading up to President Bush's announcement about his own temporary worker proposal, his administration and Congress had agreed not to maintain the higher cap for H-1B non-immigrants that had been enacted in 2000 under the American Competitiveness in the 21st Century Act (AC21). That cap had been set at 195,000 H-1B visas per year, but in the fiscal year beginning in October of 2003, that cap would fall back to 65,000 visas per year.[5] That is, the H-1B cap would revert back to the level where it had been set in the Act of 1990. Of course, the additional protections to H-1B workers would remain in force as they were enacted in AC21 and in the Competitiveness Act of 1998, but to the extent that policy makers in the United States no longer saw these workers as "necessary," their numbers would be shifted downward to satisfy a less compelling level of demand in the American labor market.

The thousands of Asian professionals who were part of a "brain circulation" into and out of the United States would have to circulate elsewhere, at least for a while. That 130,000 fewer persons would be allowed to enter the United States for employment was a relatively quiet political issue, precisely because these were "non-immigrants." Other non-immigrant employment visas, notably the "L" for intra-company transfers, would draw greater publicity, even though a much smaller number of persons were admitted under the L than under the H-1B.[6]

Yet this decision could stir anxieties among H-1B beneficiaries already in the United States. The rules in 1998 and 2000 protected these workers to some degree against labor abuse, or against bureaucratic delays in their petitions for permanent residency, but the fundamental relationship between labor and residency has remained the same. Without employment, they would have to leave the United States. Even if they had filed any kind of petition for permanent residency, there was no guarantee that the United States Citizenship and Immigration Services (one of the successor agencies to the Immigration and Naturalization Services) would grant in their favor. If they were petitioning for status as employment-based immigrants, they needed not just an employer to sponsor that petition, but also a visa to be made available from their country of origin. If they were from Asia (as most of them were) this was much less likely to happen.

Never have so many people living and working legally in the United States been under such a precarious and probationary status, where a single job conferred so directly the ability to stay or leave. Although H-1B workers have in recent years participated in the political process to improve their legal status, no amount of lobbying has changed this basic fact: that without employment, they must leave. What appears as a "flexible" rule from the perspective of the state—a rule that allows central-ized regulation of skilled employment—must at the same time leave the residual feeling among many migrant workers that they are, ultimately, an easily expendable resource that can also be "deleted."

THE ANXIETIES OF PROBATIONARY STATUS

At first glance, Mexican and Cambodian deportees, poorer immigrants seeking family reunification, and highly skilled non-immigrants would not seem to have much in common. However, their status, rights, and opportunities in the United States are all shaped by a set of immigration rules that represent a triumph of the language of the market. In many respects, the immigration law is hostile to all contemporary immigrants because it most often treats them as "costs" that need to be "reduced" or "removed," not as persons who are members of families, or as persons deserving of the same level of dignity and respect afforded to citizens. In the confluence of criminal law and immigration law, for example, immi-grants facing criminal convictions are "removed" in a formal sense, but it would be more accurate to say that the United States exports more of its criminal population than ever before. The example of Southeast Asian deportees is particularly instructive because most of these people were children when they were first admitted, and most grew up in quintessen-tially poorer American neighborhoods. The United States removes them to Southeast Asia not so much because they aren't "Americans," but chiefly because the law strives to avoid the costs associated with such people, even if that means imposing these costs on other, poorer countries.

In the same way, by discouraging family reunification for poorer immigrants, the set of laws since 1996 attempt to reduce costs more than anything else. Ostensibly, the rules make sure that all prospective sponsors are aware that they must be "responsible" for their family beneficiaries, and the family beneficiaries are themselves told that they cannot rely on public assistance. But the end result of these rules is that family reunification is a privilege that far fewer families can now afford. The law has abandoned the principle that all legal residents of the United States should have the right to be reunited with their families. Instead, the new principle would be that only those who are relatively well off should even consider family reunification. Congress favored this second principle because it was much less expensive than the first, and that decision has most adversely impacted Mexican, Central American, and Asian immigrant families.

Finally, for several years after the Act of 1990, influential policymakers favored the growth of employment-based migration to serve the nation's economic interests. This meant that immigration rules needed to protect American labor from unfair foreign competition, while at the same time providing for skilled and talented workers from abroad to grow the nation's economy.[7] Striking this balance proved exceedingly difficult, and when faced with an unprecedented demand for labor in a vital sector of the American economy, Congress chose to increase "temporary" worker categories, and only for brief periods of time. Even though substantial numbers of workers would arrive and adjust into permanent residency, the category itself was much more flexible than for permanent visa categories based on employment. This was because once permanent residency was granted, one simply could not be removed from the labor market even if there were a downturn in the economy. Non-immigrant beneficiaries—about two thirds of whom were from Asia—were subject to the same labor certification requirements as permanent residents, but their status as "non-immigrants" left them with much less security, even after favorable revisions to the law in 1998 and 2000. When there was a recent sustained downturn in the economy, Congress simply readjusted.

All these policies may have increased the state's efficient management of immigration, but they leave all immigrants in a much more vulnerable position, especially those who were admitted into the United States after 1996. These immigrants are the ones who can no longer rely on most public assistance programs, and they are the ones who can easily be removed for a criminal conviction. Of those who came for employment, a much greater fraction were "temporary" immigrants whose legal status in the United States hinged directly on their continuing employment with an

American company. These persons are the ones most likely to feel the sense of anxiety that contemporary immigration rules bring to bear.

For immigrants who have been in the United States longer, there is the option of naturalization. As most students of immigration trends already know, naturalization rates have jumped dramatically in recent years, especially after 1994 and 1996. In their own reports on naturalization trends, public officials conceded the influence of public law: "an unknown number of immigrants naturalized in response to legislative efforts restricting public benefits for the non-citizen population, including Proposition 187 in California (1994), the Personal Responsibility and Work Opportunity Act (1996), and the Illegal Immigration Reform and Immigrant Responsibility Act (1996)."[8]

Some instructive numbers for naturalization are shown in Table 8.1.

The number of naturalization petitions increased rapidly, from 342,269 in 1992 to 543,353 in 1994, and then to 1.27 million in 1996. By 1996, there were more immigrants seeking naturalization than there were public officials to adjudicate their petitions: huge backlogs formed, and only recently have they been reduced, which explains why, since 1999, more petitions have been approved in a given year than were filed during that same year. A tremendous number of immigrants in the United States have sought citizenship, perhaps because so many sensed how their immigration status left them so vulnerable. Asians were no exception: "Asian immigrants [had] had historically higher naturalization rates than other immigrants," but "since 2001, Asia has been the leading region of naturalizations." "In 2002, 41 percent of persons naturalizing were born in Asian countries compared to thirty percent for North American countries."[9]

Some critics complained that recent immigrants were becoming citizens "not out of a sense of cultural affinity, but as a means of ensuring their material future."[10] But anxieties related to other bad things that might happen as an immigrant might have been even more compelling: American citizens are not "removed" to another country, for instance, for a drunken driving conviction, or for a single conviction for shoplifting, or for losing their jobs.[11]

The numbers in Table 8.1 also show the dramatic increase in the numbers of petitions denied. To naturalize successfully, there are certain requirements: one must be at least eighteen years old; one must be a lawfully admitted permanent resident, and one must have also resided continuously in the United States for at least five years. Other requirements include rudimentary proficiency in English, basic knowledge of United States history and government, and "good moral character," which usually means the absence of any significant criminal convictions.[12] Some

TABLE 8.1 Petitions for Naturalization

Year	Petitions filed	Petitions granted	Petitions denied	Percent denied
1968	103,085	102,726	1,962	1.87%
1970	114,760	110,399	1,979	1.76%
1980	192,230	157,938	4,370	2.69%
1990	233,843	270,101	6,516	2.36%
1991	206,668	308,058	6,268	1.99%
1992	342,269	240,252	19,293	7.43%
1993	522,298	314,681	39,931	11.26%
1994	543,353	434,107	40,561	8.55%
1995	959,963	488,088	46,067	8.62%
1996	1,277,403	1,044,689	229,842	18.03%
1997	1,412,712	598,225	130,676	17.93%
1998	932,957	463,060	137,395	22.88%
1999	765,346	839,944	379,993	31.15%
2000	460,916	888,788	399,670	31.02%
2001	501,646	608,205	218,326	26.41%

Source: Immigration and Naturalization Service, *2001 Statistical Yearbook* 204 (2002).

exemptions to these requirements may apply for immediate family members, but the overall requirements for naturalization have remained consistent since the Immigration and Nationality Act of 1952.[13]

More than any of the other requirements, the requirement for "good moral character," which has become synonymous with an absence of a criminal conviction, is a much more loaded requirement for potential American citizens who desire to pass into citizenship. Less than three percent of naturalization petitions were denied before 1991, a figure that had not changed for fifty years. However, since 1992, the rate of denial grew dramatically, rising to seven percent and then to about twenty-five to thirty percent each year since 1998. This pattern was suggestive of the changing role of the former Immigration Service, now under the control of the Department of Homeland Security. Petitioners for naturalization usually find the language barrier the most difficult, but all petitioners are much more likely to undergo a thorough criminal background check than in the past. After the Supreme Court's decision in *St. Cyr*, a finding of a past criminal conviction won't necessarily lead to removal, but it will still disqualify a person from passing into citizenship. For immigrants who arrived after *St. Cyr*, however, they should be reminded of the admonition issued by the Southeast Asia Resource Action Center in 1996: even when they intend to embrace the nation through naturalization, immigrants should approach the United States only with great caution.

Endnotes

Chapter 1

1. Chew Heong, 112 U.S. 536, 569 (1884), Justice Stephen Field, dissenting.
2. Popular books on immigration are numerous, and a sample would include: Peter Brimelow, *Alien Nation: Common Sense about America's Immigration Disaster* (1996); Michelle Malkin, *Invasion: How America Still Welcomes Terrorists, Criminals, and Other Foreign Menaces to Our Shores* (2002); Victor Hanson, *Mexifornia: A State of Becoming* (2003); Patrick Buchanan, *The Death of the West: How Dying Populations and Immigrant Invasion Imperil Our Country and Civilization* (2001); Richard Lamm and Gary Imhoff, *The Immigration Time Bomb: The Fragmenting of America* (1986); and Arthur Schlesinger, *The Disuniting of America: Reflections on a Multicultural Society* (1998).
3. There is now an extensive scholarly literature, and only the most recent examples are listed here, by academic field. In economics, see: Philip Martin, *Promise Unfulfilled: Unions, Immigration, and the Farm Workers* (2003); George Borjas, *Heaven's Door: Immigration Policy and the American Economy* (2001); and Annalee Saxenian, *Silicon Valley's New Immigrant Entrepreneurs* (1999). In sociology and anthropology, see: Frank Bean and Gillian Stevens, *America's Newcomers and the Dynamics of Diversity* (2003); Aiwha Ong, *Buddha Is Hiding: Refugees, Citizenship, and New America* (2003); and Peggy Levitt, *Transnational Villagers* (2001). In urban studies, see Jennifer Lee: *Civility in the City: Blacks, Jews, and Koreans in Urban America* (2002); Saskia Sassen, *Guests and Aliens* (1999); Roger Waldinger, *Still the Promised City?: African Americans and New Immigrants in Postindustrial New York* (1999); and Michael Jones-Correa, *Between Two Nations: The Political Predicament of Latinos in New York City* (1998). In law, see: Kevin Johnson, *The "Huddled Masses" Myth: Immigration and Civil Rights* (2003); Thomas Aleinikoff, *Semblances of Sovereignty: The Constitution, the State, and American Citizenship* (2002); and Peter Schuck, *Citizens, Strangers, and In-Betweens: Essays on Immigration and Citizenship* (1998). In political science, see: Cheryl Shanks, *Immigration and the Politics Of American Sovereignty, 1890–1990* (2001); Roxanne Doty, *Anti-Immigrantism in Western Democracies: Statecraft, Desire, and the Politics of Exclusion* (2003); Vernon Briggs, *Mass Migration and the National Interest: Policy Directions for the New Century* (2003); and David Reimers, *Unwelcome Strangers: American Identity and the Turn against Immigration* (1999). In political theory, see Mai Ngai, *Impossible Subjects: Illegal Aliens and the Making of Modern America* (2004); Peter Meilander, *Toward a Theory of Immigration* (2001); Phillip Cole, *Philosophies of Exclusion* (2001); Christian Joppke, *Challenge to the Nation-State: Immigration in Western Europe and the United States* (1998); and Stephen Castles, *Ethnicity and Globalization* (2000). In literary theory, especially with respect to Asians, see: David Palumbo-Liu, *Asian/American: Historical Crossings of a Racial Frontier* (1999); Robert Lee, *Orientals: Asian Americans in Popular Culture* (1999); and Lisa Lowe, *Immigrant Acts: on Asian American Cultural Politics* (1996).

In history, see: Xiaojian Zhao, *Remaking Chinese America: Immigration, Family, and Community, 1940–1965* (2003); Erika Lee, *At America's Gate: Chinese Immigration During The Exclusion Era, 1882–1943* (2003); and Roger Daniels and Otis Graham, *Debating American Immigration, 1882–Present* (2001).

4. See Saxenian, supra note 3.
5. Immigration and Naturalization Service, *2001 Statistical Yearbook* Table 62 (2002).
6. There are other compelling reasons: since Chinese Exclusion, Congress has had "plenary power" over immigration, meaning that the federal courts and executive officials typically defer to Congress in broad matters of immigration policy. For a helpful discussion of the history of this power and its development in the immigration law, both with regard to the federal courts and executive officials, see: Lucy Salyer, *Laws Harsh as Tigers: Chinese Immigrants and the Shaping of Modern Immigration Law* (1995).

Chapter 2

1. Declaration of Independence (1776). Jefferson continued: "He has excited domestic insurrections amongst us, and has endeavoured to bring on the inhabitants of our frontiers, the merciless Indian Savages, whose known rule of warfare, is an undistinguished destruction of all ages, sexes and conditions."
2. U.S. Constitution, art. I, §9.
3. Gerald Neuman, *Strangers to the Constitution: Immigrants, Borders, and Fundamental Law* (1996).
4. Ronald Takaki, *Strangers from a Different Shore: A History of Asian Americans* (1989); Charles McClain, *In Search of Equality: The Chinese Struggle against Discrimination in Nineteenth-Century America* (1996); Sucheng Chan, *Asian Americans: An Interpretive History* (1991); Lucy Salyer, *Laws Harsh as Tigers: Chinese Immigrants and the Shaping of Modern Immigration Law* (1995); Andrew Gyory, *Closing the Gate: Race, Politics, and the Chinese Exclusion Act* (1998); Robert Lee: *Orientals: Asian Americans in Popular Culture* (2000); Desmond King, *Making Americans: Immigration, Race, and the Origins of the Diverse Democracy* (2002); and Erika Lee, *At America's Gates: Chinese Immigration during the Exclusion Era, 1882–1943* (2003).
5. John Higham, *Strangers in the Land: Patterns of American Nativism, 1860–1925* (1955, 2002). Other excellent monographs on this period would include: Oscar Handlin, *The Uprooted* (1973); Roger Daniels: *Not Like Us: Immigrants and Minorities in America, 1890–1924* (1998); Matthew Frye Jacobson, *Barbarian Virtues: The United States Encounters Foreign Peoples at Home and Abroad, 1876–1917* (2001); and Robert Wiebe, *The Search for Order, 1877–1920* (1980).
6. For a useful biography of Stanford, see Norman Tutorow, *Leland Stanford: Man of Many Careers* (1971).
7. Higham, supra note 5.
8. See, for example, an account of Henry Ford's efforts in James Barrett, "Americanization from the Bottom Up: Immigration and the Remaking of the Working Class in the United States, 1880–1930," 79 *J. Amer. Hist.* 996 (1992).
9. Higham, supra note 5, 317.
10. For a scholarly discussion of this intervening period, see Robert Divine, *American Immigration Policy, 1924–1952* (1957).
11. President's Commission on Immigration and Naturalization, "Whom We Shall Welcome" (1953).
12. See, generally, Frank Auerbach and Elizabeth Harper, *Immigration Laws of the United States* ch. 14 (3rd ed., 1975).
13. INA, §203(a)(3) and (6).
14. INA, §203(a)(3) and (6).
15. The Brain Drain into the United States of Scientists, Engineers, and Physicians. Report to the House Committee on Government Operations, Research and Technical Programs Subcommittee (1967). Congressional testimony on the migration of skilled workers was presented to the Senate Judiciary Committee in spring of that same year.
16. Takaki, supra note 4, 434, 437, and 439.

17. National Science Foundation, *Immigrant Scientists and Engineers: 1990* (1993). See also, Charles Keely, "Effects of U.S. Immigration Law on Manpower Characteristics of Immigrants", 12 *Demography* 179 (1975), Wilawan Kanjanapan, "The Immigration of Asian Professionals to the United States, 1988–1990," 29 *Int. Mig. Rev.* 7 (1995), Jessica Gurcak, Thomas Espenshade, Aaron Sparrow, and Martha Paskoff, "Immigration of Scientists and Engineers to the United States: Issues and Evidence", in *The International Migration of the Highly Skilled: Demand, Supply, and Development Consequences in Sending and Receiving Countries* (Wayne Cornelius, Thomas Espenshade, and Idean Salehyan, Eds., 2001); and Joyce Tang, *Doing Engineering: The Career Attainment and Mobility of Caucasian, Black, and Asian-American Engineers* (2000).

18. On popular images of Asian Americans from 1960 to 1990, see: Keith Osajima, "Asian Americans as the Model Minority: An Analysis of the Popular Press Image in the 1960s and 1980s", reprinted in *Contemporary Asian America: A Multidisciplinary Reader* ch. 19 (2000).

19. On the Immigration Act of 1965 generally, see: David Reimers, *Still the Golden Door: The Third World Comes to America* (1985, 1992). This volume remains the best account of the history and consequences of the Act of 1965. For further discussions of the legislative intent behind the Act of 1965, see: Gabriel Chin, "The Civil Rights Revolution Comes to Immigration Law: A New Look at the Immigration and Nationality Act of 1965," 75 *N.C.L. Rev.* 273 (1996).

20. See Juan Ramon Garcia, *Operation Wetback: The Mass Deportation Of Mexican Undocumented Workers in 1954* (1980), and Kitty Calavita, *Inside The State: The Bracero Program, Immigration, and the I.N.S.* (1992). See also the discussion in Chapter 6. For excellent histories of Mexican Americans in the border states before the Act of 1965, see: Tomas Almaguer, *Racial Fault Lines: Historical Origins of White Supremacy in California* (1994); George Sanchez, *Becoming Mexican American: Ethnicity, Culture, and Identity in Chicano Los Angeles, 1900–1945* (1995); Neil Foley, *The White Scourge: Mexicans, Blacks, and Poor Whites in Texas Cotton Culture* (1999); and Sarah Jane Deutsch, *No Separate Refuge: Culture, Class, and Gender on an Anglo-Hispanic Frontier in the American Southwest, 1880–1940* (1989).

21. For thorough studies of the 1986 Act and its limited success, see: *Undocumented Migration to the United States: The Immigration Reform and Control Act and the Experience of the 1980s* (Frank Bean, Barry Edmonston, and Jeffrey Passel, Eds., 1990); Susan Gonzalez Baker, *The Cautious Welcome: The Legalization Programs of the Immigration Reform and Control Act* (1990); Peter Schuck, "The Politics of Rapid Legal Change: Immigration Policy in the 1980s," 6 *Stud. Amer. Pol. Dev.* 40 (1992); and Lawrence Fuchs, "The Corpse That Would Not Die: The Immigration Reform and Control Act of 1986," 6 *Rev. Européenne des Mig. Int.* 124 (1990). Figures for legal adjustments under the Immigration Reform and Control Act come from David Reimers, *Unwelcome Strangers: American Identity and the Turn against Immigration,* 26–28 (1998).

22. Keller v. United States, 213 U.S. 138 (1909).

23. *Id.*

24. *Id.* at 148. For Brewer, not acknowledging such a limit would have extended the federal government beyond all reasonable bounds, on 148–149: "If that be possible, the door is open to the assumption by the National Government of an almost unlimited body of legislation. By the census of 1900 the population of the United States between the oceans was in round numbers 76,000,000. Of these, 10,000,000 were of foreign birth, and 16,000,000 more were of foreign parentage. Doubtless some have become citizens by naturalization, but certainly scattered through the country there are millions of aliens. If the contention of the Government be sound, whatever may have been done in the past, however little this field of legislation may have been entered upon, the power of Congress is broad enough to cognizance of all dealings of citizens with aliens. That there is a moral consideration of the special facts of this case, that the act charged is within the scope of the police power, is immaterial, for, as stated, there is in the Constitution no grant to Congress of the police power.... Although Congress has not largely entered into this field of legislation, it may do so, if it has the power."

25. See, for example, American Friends Service Corporation v. Thornburgh, 961 F.2d 1405, 1406 (9th Cir. 1991). More recent decisions tend to acknowledge that although undocumented workers are "employees," when they seek relief under the National Labor Relations Act, for example, they are still subject to deportation even though they may be harmed by

unfair labor practices. See, for example, Hoffman Plastic Compounds, Inc. v. National Labor Relations Board, 535 U.S. 137 (2002); and Sure-Tan, Inc. v. National Labor Relations Board, 467 U.S. 883 (1984).

26. Pub. L. 101–649, §§541–544.

27. For a discussion of the legislative intent behind the Act of 1990, see *Legislative History of the Immigration Act of 1990, Public Law 101–649* (Igor Kavass and Bernard Reams, Eds., 1997).

28. Ji-Yeon Yuh, *Beyond the Shadow of Camptown: Korean Military Brides in America* 164 (2002).

29. Technically, the second preference is subdivided into 2A and 2B—2A covers spouses and minor children, 2B covers children over 21 years of age. The statute further requires that 2B admits cannot exceed 23% of all immigrants coming under the second preference.

30. Stephen Legomsky, *Immigration Law and Policy* 138 (1992).

31. For a discussion of some of these debates, see *Understanding the Immigration Act of 1990* (Stephen Yale-Loehr, Ed., 1991); and Richard Lamm and Gary Imhoff, *The Immigration Time Bomb: The Fragmenting of America* 24–25 (1985). Subsequent discussions about the shift in emphasis in immigration law can be found in: *Blueprints for an Ideal Immigration Policy* (Richard Lamm and Alan Simpson, Eds., 2001).

32. For an analysis of the political campaign in favor of Proposition 187, see Kent Ono and John Sloop, *Shifting Borders: Rhetoric, Immigration, and California's Proposition 187* (2002).

33. Reimers, supra note 19, ch. 7. For background and commentary on Proposition 187, see John SW Park, note, "Race Discourse and Proposition 187," 2 *Mich. J. Race & L.* 175 (1996).

34. Pub. L. 101–649, at §§121 and 216.

35. *Id.*, at §536; see also 8 U.S.C. 1324, an entire section of the United States Code that promises in rather threatening and ominous language very severe civil and criminal penalties (including forfeiture) for anyone who violates the labor certification processes or other immigration procedures in favor of an alien.

36. Stephen Legomsky, "*Immigration, Equality and Diversity,*" 31 *Colum. J. Transnat'l L.* 319 329–30 (1993). Legomsky continued, on 334: "The fallacy [of the diversity visa] lies in the unspoken assumption that diversifying the *immigrant stream* will somehow diversify the *resulting United States population*. In truth, exactly the opposite is the case. Since more Americans already trace their ancestries to Europe than to Latin America or Asia, any program that increases the European proportion of the immigrant stream makes the resulting United States population less diverse—not more diverse—than it would otherwise be."

37. Kevin Johnson, "*Race and the Immigration Laws: The Need for Critical Inquiry,*" in *Crossroads, Directions, and a New Critical Race Theory* 187, 193 (Francisco Valdes et al. Eds., 2002). See also, Victor Romero, "Critical Race Theory in Three Acts: Racial Profiling, Affirmative Action, and the Diversity Visa Lottery," 66 *Alb. L. Rev.* 375 (2003).

38. See Immigration and Naturalization Service's *Statistical Yearbooks*, esp. from 1998, 1999, 2000, and 2001. In 1999, about 7,000 diversity visas went to Asians, while Africans received 15,000 and Europeans received over 22,000. It would seem that initially, Europeans were in a better position to discover these visas than either Asians or Africans. In more recent years, the gap between Europeans and Africans has decreased.

39. See Romero, supra note 37.

40. *Id.*

Chapter 3

1. Pub. L. 101–649, §601.

2. For a fascinating account of public health issues arising from San Francisco Chinatown, see Nayan Shah, *Contagious Divides: Epidemics and Race in San Francisco Chinatown* (2001), and Charles McClain, *In Search of Equality: The Chinese Struggle against Discrimination in Nineteenth-Century America* ch. 10 (1996).

3. For a general history of this period, see Daniel Kevles, *In the Name of Eugenics: Genetics and the Uses of Human Heredity* (1998).

4. Boutilier v. INS, 387 U.S. 118 (1967).

5. See generally, Stephen Legomsky, *Immigration and Refugee Law and Policy* ch. 4, §C (2nd ed., 1997).

6. Nelson Mandela, *Long Walk to Freedom* 507 (1994).
7. In July of 2003, the *Los Angeles Times* reported a story about a tourist arriving at Los Angeles International Airport from Belgium—she was sent back to Belgium after fifteen hours of detention and a full search of her belongings and person, and all this because she did not have a new, machine-readable passport. Her children and another traveling companion from France had these new passports, so they waited twelve days for her return to Los Angeles with her new passport. For this story, see: Jean Pasco, "Locked Up at LAX Over Passport Policy," *L.A. Times* (Jul. 5, 2003).
8. Gerald Neuman, *Strangers to the Constitution: Immigrants, Borders, and Fundamental Law* ch. 2 (1996).
9. See, generally, Leon Litwack, *North of Slavery: The Negro in the Free States, 1790–1860* (1961).
10. See John Higham, *Strangers in the Land: Patterns of American Nativism, 1860–1925* (1955, 2002); Lucy Salyer, *Laws Harsh as Tigers: Chinese Immigrants and the Shaping of Modern Immigration Law* (1995); and United States ex rel. Smith v. Curran, 12 F. 2d 636 (1926).
11. Department of Mental Hygiene of the State of California v. Renel, 167 N.Y.S. 2d 22, 30, 23 (1957)
12. Department of Mental Hygiene of the State of California v. Renel, 167 N.Y.S. 2d 28, 26 (1957).
13. Department of Mental Hygiene of the State of California v. Renel, 173 N.Y.S. 2d 231 (1958).
14. State v. Binder, 96 N.W. 2d 140 (1959), and County of San Diego v. Viloria, 276 Cal. App. 2d 350 (1969). In this second case, the California Court of Appeals noted the differences between an affidavit of support and a formal contract: "The writing is entitled 'Affidavit of Support' not 'Contract of Support' nor an 'Agreement of Support'; is signed only by the affiant; does not recite or disclose a consideration; is a form supplied by an undisclosed source; in major parts contains statements of an evidentiary nature, added to the form, respecting the affiant's citizenship, marital status, property ownership and income; and in only two lines sets forth the form language upon which plaintiff [the County of San Diego] relies as the basis for a contractual obligation." also at 357.
15. 276 Cal. App. 2d, at 360.
16. Charles Reich, "The New Property," 73 *Yale L. J.* 933 (1964).
17. For example, see: Graham v. Richardson, 403 U.S. 365 (1971) [concerning welfare eligibility for legal immigrants]; and Plyler v. Doe, 457 U.S. 202 (1982) [concerning the constitutionality of Texas rules denying free primary public schooling to undocumented aliens].
18. See INA, §241(a)(5).
19. Michael Sheridan, "The New Affidavit of Support and Other 1996 Amendments to Immigration and Welfare Provisions Designed to Prevent Aliens from Becoming Public Charges", 31 *Creighton L. Rev.* 741, 743 (1998).
20. For a concise discussion of the exclusion and deportation of "political undesirables," see Kevin Johnson, *The "Huddled Masses" Myth: Immigration and Civil Rights* (2004); On McKinley, his assassin, and the subsequent political fallout see, Eric Rauchway, *Murdering McKinley: The Making of Theodore Roosevelt's America* (2003).
21. For examples of deportation cases testing these laws, see: Turner v. Williams, 194 U.S. 279 (1904); Guiney v. Bonham, 261 F. 582 (9th Cir. 1919); and Tisi v. Tod, 264 U.S. 131 (1924). Other dramatic cases involving ideological exclusion, including Bridges v. Wixon, 326 U.S. 135 (1945), Knauff v. Shaughnessy, 338 U.S. 537 (1950), United States v. Mezei, 345 U.S. 208 (1953), Galvan v. Press, 347 U.S. 522 (1954), and Jay v. Boyd, 351 U.S. 345 (1956), are discussed in Johnson, supra note 20, ch. 3.
22. The quote is from Xiaojian Zhao, *Remaking Chinese America: Immigration, Family, and Community, 1940–1965* 168 (2002). For more historical background on the "Confession Program," under which federal authorities promised amnesty to undocumented Chinese aliens who cooperated with federal investigators in identifying and locating leftist Chinese Americans, see: Victor Nee and Brett De Bary Nee, *Longtime Californ': A Documentary Study of an American Chinatown* (1973); Mae Ngai, "Legacies of Exclusion: Illegal Chinese Immigration During the Cold War Years," 18 *J. Amer. Ethn. Hist.* 1 (1998); and Mae Ngai, *Impossible Subjects: Illegal Aliens and the Making of Modern America* (2003).
23. Immigration and Naturalization Service, *2001 Statistical Yearbook* Tables 62, 63, and 64 (2002).

24. Bugajewitz v. Adams, 228 U.S. 585, 591 (1913).
25. For an excellent scholarly discussion of the distinction between civil procedure and criminal procedure in immigration law, see Hiroshi Motomura, "*Immigration Law After a Century of Plenary Power: Phantom Constitutional Norms and Statutory Interpretation*," 100 *Yale L.J.* 545 (1990).
26. See, for example, Ng Fung Ho v. White, 259 U.S. 276 (1922).
27. Ng Fung Ho v. White, 259 U.S. 284 (1922).
28. Fong Haw Tan v. Phelan, 333 U.S. 6, 10 (1948): "We resolve the doubts in favor of that construction because deportation is a drastic measure and at times the equivalent of banishment or exile .... It is the forfeiture for misconduct of a residence in this country. Such a forfeiture is a penalty. To construe this statutory provision less generously to the alien might find support in logic. But since the stakes are considerable for the individual, we will not assume that the Congress meant to trench on his freedom beyond that which is required by the narrowest of several possible meanings of the words used."
29. Pub. L. 101–649, §§501–515.
30. See generally, *The Oxford History of the Prison: The Practice of Punishment in Western Society* (Norval Morris and David Rothman, 1997); and Elizabeth Vodola, *Excommunication in the Middle Ages* (1986).
31. For historical background on American refugee policies, see: David Wyman, *Paper Walls: America and the Refugee Crisis, 1938–1941* (1968); James Hathaway, *The Law of Refugee Status* (1991); Naomi Zucker and Norman Zucker, *The Guarded Gate: The Reality of American Refugee Policy* (1987); Gil Loescher and John Scanlan, *Calculated Kindness: Refugees and America's Half-Open Door, 1945 to the Present* (1986); and Deborah Anker and Michael Posner, "The Forty Year Crisis: A Legislative History of the Refugee Act of 1980", 1 *San Diego L. Rev.* 9 (1981).
32. See generally, Stephen Legomsky, *Immigration and Refugee Law and Policy* (2nd ed., 1997).
33. See generally, Philip Schrag, *A Well-Founded Fear: The Congressional Battle to Save Political Asylum in America* (2000).
34. Immigration and Naturalization Service, supra note 23, Table 8; Office of the United Nations High Commissioner for Refugees, *The State of the World's Refugees, 1997–1998: A Humanitarian Agenda* (1997); and Office of the United Nations High Commissioner for Refugees, *Refugees* (2003).
35. The phrase is from former Senator Alan Simpson, quoted in David Simcox, *U.S. Immigration in the 1980s: Reappraisal and Reform* (1988).
36. Immigration and Naturalization Service, supra note 23, Table 30.
37. United States Department Of Commerce, *United States Census 2000: The Asian Population, 2000* Table 4 (2002)
38. Immigration and Naturalization Service, supra note 23, Table 21.
39. Bill Ong Hing, *Making and Remaking Asian America through Immigration Policy, 1850–1990* 137 (1994).
40. See generally, Sucheng Chan and Audrey Kim, *Not Just Victims: Conversations with Cambodian Community Leaders in the United States* (2003); and Sucheng Chan, *Hmong Means Free: Life in Laos and America* (1994).
41. See generally, Hien Duc Do, *The Vietnamese Americans* (2000); James Freeman, *Hearts of Sorrow: Vietnamese American Lives* (1991); and Min Zhou and Carl Bankston, *Growing Up American: How Vietnamese Children Adapt to Life in the United States* (1998).
42. Schrag, supra note 33; James Hathaway and R. Alexander Neve, "Making International Refugee Law Relevant Again: A Proposal for Collectivized and Solution-Oriented Protection," 10 *Harv. Hum. Rts. J.* 115 (1997).
43. See, for example, "Guo Chun Di v. Carroll: The Refugee Status of Chinese Nationals Fleeing Persecution Resulting from China's Coercive Population Control Measures," 20 *N.C.J. Int. L. & Com. Reg.* 685 (1995).
44. "*International and Domestic Political Developments Spark Debate Over Future of Refugee Resettlement Program*," *Refugee Rep.* 1, 3 (U.S. Committee for Refugees, Washington, D.C., June 30, 1994).
45. On the Commission and its series of reports, see: Carlos Miranda, "United States Commission on Immigration Reform: The Interim and Final Reports," 38 *Santa Clara L. Rev.* 645 (1998). For reviews of Barbara Jordan's political history and biography, see Mary Beth

Rogers, *Barbara Jordan: American Hero* (2000); and Barbara Jordan, *Selected Speeches* (1999). Barbara Jordan has testified several times to Congress, but one instance where she mentions welfare policy and refugee policy is: Barbara Jordan, Testimony to the House Ways and Means Committee, Aug. 9, 1994.

46. See, generally, Republican National Committee, *Contract with America* (1994); for a discussion of how Congress began to implement the Contract, see James Gimpel, *Legislating Revolution: The Contract with American in Its First 100 Days* (1995).

Chapter 4

1. The phrase comes from Herbert Gans, *The War against the Poor: The Underclass and Antipoverty Policy* (1996).
2. Media coverage of this type of congressional testimony was extensive. This particular quote is from John Nuckolls, head of the Lawrence Livermore National Laboratory, in his testimony to the House Armed Services committee on March 22, 1994, quoted in David Perlman, "Lab Chief Warns of Nuclear Threat," *S.F. Chron.* (Mar. 23, 1994). See also, Karen Ball, "House Panel Hears FBI Theories on N.Y. Blast," *Chig. Sun-Times* (Mar. 10, 1993).
3. Timothy McVeigh was apprehended and charged with participating in the bombing in Oklahoma City. He was subsequently convicted and sentenced to death for the murder of 168 people. On June 11, 2001, he was executed by lethal injection, the first federal execution since 1963.
4. Pub. L. 104–132. Terrorists and their representatives are defined in §411; exclusion proceedings are defined in §422, and denial of judicial review for exclusion under these circumstances is in §423.
5. Our emphasis. The original language was in INA, §241(a)(2)(A)(i)(II); it is replaced in Pub.L. 104–132, §435.
6. Pub. L. 104–132, §439.
7. Pub. L. 104–132, §§440–442. The challenges to indefinite detention are discussed at length later in this chapter.
8. Pub. L. 104–132, §439.
9. Pub. L. 104–132, §432. The section reads: "The criminal alien identification system shall be used to assist Federal, State, and local law enforcement agencies in identifying and locating aliens who may be subject to deportation by reason of their conviction of aggravated felonies."
10. Statement of Lamar Smith, Committee on Immigration and Claims, House Judiciary Committee, Jul. 15, 1997. Representative Smith said: "After ten years of study and implementation, the IHP still has not come close to fulfilling its intended potential. Only a small minority of the eligible prisoners are actually removed pursuant to the IHP." The IHP sometimes appears as the Criminal Alien Institutional Hearing Program, its acronym appearing as CAP.
11. Daniel Kanstroom, "Deportation, Social Control, and Punishment: Some Thoughts About Why Hard Laws Make Bad Cases," 113 *Harv. L. Rev.* 1889, 1891 (2000). See also, Elwin Griffith, "The Transition Between Suspension of Deportation and Cancellation of Removal for Non-Permanent Residents Under the Immigration and Nationality Act: The Impact of the 1996 Reform Legislation," 48 *Drake L. Rev.* 79 (1999).
12. The language comes from the Alien Registration Act of 1940, ch. 439, quoted in Griffith, supra note 11, 81–82.
13. Immigration and Nationality Act of 1952, §244(a). For examples of some of this litigation, see: Bastidas v. Immigration and Naturalization Service, 609 F.2d 101 (3rd Cir. 1979); Immigration and Naturalization Service v. Jung Ha Wang, 450 U.S. 139 (1981); Hee Yung Ahn v. Immigration and Naturalization Service, 651 F.2d 1285 (9th Cir. 1981); and Antoine-Dorcelli v. Immigration and Naturalization Service, 703 F.2d 19 (1st Cir. 1983).
14. The case, United States ex rel. Klonis v. Davis, 13 F.2d 630, 630-631 (2nd Cir. 1926), was brought to our attention in the first page of the article by Kanstroom, supra note 11.
15. Griffith, supra note 11, 134.
16. Smith, supra note 10.

17. In classic immigration law, an alien is only "admitted" when federal authorities expressly grant him the right to enter. Persons who come to the United States but do not have such permission are not regarded as having been legally "admitted." See, for example, Matter of Kazemi, 19 I. & N. Dec. 49 (BIA, 1984), as well as INA § 235(b).

18. Michael Pistone and Philip Schrag, "The New Asylum Rule: Improved But Still Unfair," 16 *Geo. Immigr. L. J.* 1, 9 (2001).

19. Pub. L. 104–208, all the new provisions are in Title III. For an incredibly detailed treatment of "expedited removal" and its impact on refugee and asylum claims, see: "The Expedited Removal Study: Report on the First Three Years of Implementation of Expedited Removal, pts. 1 and 2," 15 *ND J. L. Ethics & Pub. Pol'y* 1 (2001).

20. For thorough reviews of the Responsibility Act's removal provisions, see: Melissa Cook, "Banished for Minor Crimes: The Aggravated Felony Provision of the Immigration and Nationality Act as a Human Rights Violation," 23 *B.C. Third World L.J.* 293 (2003), and Timothy Mulvaney, "Categorical Approach of Categorical Chaos? A Critical Analysis of the Inconsistencies in Determining Whether Felony DWI Is a Crime of Violence for Purposes of Deportation Under 18 U.S.C. 16," 48 *Vill. L. Rev.* 697 (2003). For a political commentary, see Bill Ong Hing, "Deported for Shoplifting?" *Wash. Post* (Dec. 29, 2002).

21. See generally: Nancy Morawetz, "Rethinking Retroactive Deportation Laws and the Due Process Clause," 73 *N.Y.U. L. Rev.* 97 (1998); Peter Schuck and John Williams, "Removing Criminal Aliens: The Pitfalls and Promises of Federalism," 22 *Harv. J. L. & Pub. Pol'y* 367 (1999); Iris Bennett, "The Unconstitutionality of Non-Uniform Immigration Consequences of 'Aggravated Felony' Convictions," 74 *N.Y.U. L. Rev.* 1696 (1999); and Bruce Marley, "Exiling the New Felons: The Consequences of the Retroactive Application of Aggravated Felony Convictions to Lawful Permanent Residents," 35 *San Diego L. Rev.* 855 (1998). See, also, Cook, supra note 20, 310: "The harsh provisions of the 1996 laws, particularly the retroactive effect of [Responsibility Act], attracted widespread media attention. Reports uncovered that the INS, pursuant to these laws, began deporting lawful permanent residents because minor crimes they had committed years before had since become aggravated felonies. For example, in 1987, twenty-one-year-old Alejandro Bontia was convicted of sexual contact with a minor for having sex with his sixteen-year-old girlfriend, because her mother was angry about the relationship and reported Mr. Bontia to the police. Almost fifteen years later, he faced separation from his wife and child solely because of this 'youthful dalliance.' Nigerian native Olufolake Olaleye became a permanent resident in 1990, and both of her children were born in the United States. She was ordered deported based on a six-year-old conviction for shoplifting baby clothes worth $14.99."

22. Nancy Morawetz, "Understanding the Impact of the 1996 Deportation Laws and the Limited Scope of Proposed Reforms," 113 *Harv. L. Rev.* 1936, 1937 (2000). Professor Moravetz continued: "In addition, changes in criminal justice policies, Immigration and Naturalization Service (INS) enforcement policies, and the new mandatory detention system render the new laws far more unforgiving in practice than is apparent from their texts. As a result, the new deportation regime greatly increases the risk that a conviction for a crime will result not only in criminal punishment, but also in exile and family separation." For additional background and discussion, see: Schuck and Williams, supra note 21.

23. See Morawetz, supra note 22, and her discussion of Mojica v. Reno, 970 F. Supp. 130 (E.D.N.Y. 1997).

24. For a discussion of how the threat of removal proceedings shapes criminal defense strategy for non-citizens, see Jennifer Welch, "Defending Against Deportation: Equipping Public Defenders to Represent Non-Citizens Effectively," 92 *Cal. L. Rev.* 541 (2004); John Francis, "Failure to Advise Non-Citizens of Immigration Consequences of Criminal Convictions: Should This Be Grounds to Withdraw a Guilty Plea?" 36 *U. Mich. J.L. Ref.* 691 (2003); and Gabriel Chin and Richard Holmes, "Effective Assistance of Counsel and the Consequences of Guilty Pleas," 87 *Cornell L. Rev.* 697 (2002).

25. For a thorough review, see Austin Fragomen, "The Illegal Immigration Reform and Immigrant Responsibility Act of 1996," 31 *Int. Migr. Rev.* 438 (1997).

26. See, for example: Robert James McWhorter, "Hell Just Got Hotter: The Rings of Immigration Hell and the Immigration Consequences to Aliens Convicted of Crimes Revisited," 11 *Geo. Immigr. L.J.* 507 (1997); Terry Coonan, "Dolphins Caught in Congressional Fishnets—Immigration Law's New Aggravated Felons," 12 *Geo. Immigr. L.J.* 589 (1998); and

Brent Newcomb, "Immigration Law and the Criminal Alien: A Comparison of Policies for Arbitrary Deportations of Legal Permanent Residents Convicted of Aggravated Felonies," 51 *Okla. L. Rev.* 697 (1998).

27. For background and discussion, see: Timothy Dunn, *The Militarization of the U.S.–Mexico Border, 1978–1992: Low-Intensity Conflict Doctrine Comes Home* (1996); Joseph Nevins and Mike Davis, *Operation Gatekeeper: The Rise of the "Illegal Alien" and the Remaking of the U.S.–Mexico Boundary* (2001); and Peter Andreas, *Border Games: Policing the U.S.–Mexico Divide* (2001).

28. See for example: Statement of Janet Reno, Attorney General, to the Senate Judiciary Committee, Mar. 14, 1995; and Statement of Doris Meissner, Commissioner of the Immigration and Naturalization Service, to the Senate Judiciary Committee, Sep. 13, 1995. Both claimed they were following the guidelines provided by the President's Commission on Immigration Reform chaired by Barbara Jordan.

29. The quote is from Wayne Cornelius, "An Immoral Policy on Illegal Entry," *L.A. Times* (June 8, 2003). This opinion piece was drawn from Professor Cornelius' earlier scholarly work: Wayne Cornelius, "Death at the Border: Efficacy and Unintended Consequences of U.S. Immigration Control Policy," 27 *Pop. & Dev. Rev.* 661 (2001). See also: Guillermo Meneses, "Human Rights and Undocumented Migration along the Mexican-U.S. Border," 51 *UCLA L. Rev.* 267, 274 (2003); Wayne Cornelius, "Death at the Border: The Efficacy and 'Unintended' Consequences of U.S. Immigration Control Policy, 1993–2000" (Center for Comparative Immigration Studies, Working Paper, 2000); and Karl Eschbach et al., "Death at the Border," 33 *Int. Mig. Rev.* 430 (1999).

30. Statement of David Martin, General Counsel, Immigration and Naturalization Service, to the House Subcommittee on Immigration and Claims, Sep. 5, 1996.

31. Statement of Anthony Moscato, Director of the Executive Office for Immigration Claims, to the House Subcommittee on Immigration and Claims, Sep. 5, 1996.

32. Statement of Doris Meissner, Commission of the Immigration and Naturalization Service, Senate Subcommittee on Immigration, Oct. 2, 1996.

33. 533 U.S at 323–324.

34. 533 U.S at 323–324, quoting *Landgraf*, 511 U.S. at 270. In part, the "*Landgraf* test" said that retroactive applications of any law should be impermissible *unless* there was clear Congressional intent to affect a retroactive application in a specific piece of legislation. Discovering the intent of Congress proved to be the central concern of several other cases concerning the retroactive applications of the Anti-Terrorism Act and the Responsibility Act. See, for example, In re QTMT, Int. Dec. #3300 (Dec. 23, 1996).

35. The dissenters said that contrary to the claims of the majority, Congress *did* state in "utterly clear" terms an intent to apply retroactively the new removal rules in the Acts of 1996, and to deny discretionary relief and judicial review in criminal deportation cases. See Scalia's dissenting opinion, 121 S. Ct., at 2293.

36. Zadvydas v. Davis, 121 S. Ct. 2491, 2495–2496 (2001). The Court continued: "Zadvydas has a long criminal record, involving drug crimes, attempted robbery, attempted burglary, and theft. He has a history of flight, from both criminal and deportation proceedings. Most recently, he was convicted of possessing, with intent to distribute, cocaine; sentenced to 16 years' imprisonment; released on parole after two years; taken into INS custody; and, in 1994, ordered deported to Germany."

37. See, for example, Phan v. Reno, 56 F. Supp. 2d 1149 (W.D. Wash. 1999), and Ho v. Greene, 204 F. 3d 1045 (10th Cir. 2000). For commentary on these and similar cases, see Gerald Neuman, "Jurisdiction and the Rule of Law After the 1996 Immigration Act," 113 *Harv. L. Rev.* 1963 (2000); Erika Anderson, "A Man Without a Country: When the Inability to Deport Becomes a Life Sentence," 24 *Hamline L. Rev.* 390 (2001); Victoria Capitaine, "Life in Prison without a Trial: The Indefinite Detention of Immigrants in the United States," 79 *Tex. L. Rev.* 769 (2001); and Jana Seng, "Cambodian Nationality Law and the Repatriation of Convicted Aliens Under the Illegal Immigration Reform and Immigrant Responsibility Act," 10 *Pac. Rim L. & Pol'y* 443 (2001).

38. Zadvydas, 121 S. Ct. at 2498–2500.

39. Zadvydas, 121 S. Ct. at 2505–2506. Breyer said: "While an argument can be made for confining any presumption to 90 days, we doubt that when Congress shortened the removal period to 90 days in 1996 it believed that all reasonably foreseeable removals could be

accomplished in that time. We do have reason to believe, however, that Congress previously doubted the constitutionality of detention for more than six months. ... Consequently, for the sake of uniform administration in the federal courts, we recognize that period. After this 6-month period, once the alien provides good reason to believe that there is no significant likelihood of removal in the reasonably foreseeable future, the Government must respond with evidence sufficient to rebut that showing. And for detention to remain reasonable, as the period of prior post-removal confinement grows, what counts as the 'reasonably foreseeable future' conversely would have to shrink. This 6-month presumption, of course, does not mean that every alien not removed must be released after six months. To the contrary, an alien may be held in confinement until it has been determined that there is no significant likelihood of removal in the reasonably foreseeable future." Since *Zadvydas*, subsequent legislation has been mindful of this standard, although security concerns since September 11th have pushed the standard further. For instance, the Patriot Act, passed in the wake of the attacks of September 11th, listed similar procedures for immigration detention, although it did give "the Attorney General the ability to detain an immigrant during the entire deportation hearing if he 'reasonably believes' the alien may have engaged or assisted in any terrorist activity." See: Mark Bastian, "The Spectrum of Certainty Left by *Zadvydas v. Davis*: Is the Alien Detention Provision of the USA Patriot Act Constitutional?" 47 *N.Y.L. Sch. L. Rev.* 395 (2003).

40. See, for example, Demore v. Kim, 538 U.S. 510 (2003).
41. Zadvydas, Kennedy's dissenting opinion, 121 S. Ct. at 2512.
42. Memorandum between the United States and the Royal Government of Cambodia for the Establishment and Operation of a United States–Cambodia Joint Commission on Repatriation, Mar. 22, 2002. The Memorandum is signed by United States Ambassador Kent Wiedermann and Lieutenant General Em Sam An, the Secretary of the Ministry of Interior. Consider this news report, published in *Newsweek*: "Cambodian officials claim they were strong-armed into signing the agreement. A senior Cambodian official indicated that Phnom Penh's acceptance of the terms was linked in their minds to vital World Bank and IMF assistance, which would be torpedoed by diplomatic pressure from Washington. 'If we don't have help from behind the scenes from the United States, how could we get assistance?' says the senior official. The Cambodian government also claims that had it not gone along, the U.S. Attorney General could have imposed a number of sanctions, including freezing visas to the United States." Joe Cochrane and Adam Piore, "A Bitter Bon-Voyage," *Newsweek* (Aug. 5, 2002).
43. Southeast Asia Resource Action Center, Press Release, "United States, Cambodian Governments Plan to Force Refugees Back to Cambodia" (May 7, 2002).
44. See, generally: David Chandler, *A History of Cambodia* (2000); Elizabeth Becker, *When the War Was Over: Cambodia and the Khmer Rouge Revolution* (1998); and Pierre Lizee, *Peace, Power, and Resistance in Cambodia: Global Governance and the Failure of International Conflict Resolution* (1999). For background on the children of Cambodian refugees, see *Children of Cambodia's Killing Fields: Memoirs by Survivors* (Dith Tran et al, Eds., 1999).
45. See Seth Mydans, "Dead End for Cambodians Who Grew So American," *New York Times* (Aug. 9, 2002), and Kermit Pattison, "Deportee Impact Ignites Wider Fear," *Pioneer Press* (Aug. 11, 2002).
46. Lourdes Leslie, "Treaty Stirs Anxieties in Cambodians," *Star Trib.* (Sep. 16, 2002); Teresa Watanabe, "Cambodians Fear Possible Deportation," *L.A. Times* (Feb. 21, 2003); and Richard Paddock, "Cambodia's Black Sheep Return to Fold," *L.A. Times* (Mar. 28, 2003).
47. 2001 Bill Tracking H.R. 1452, The Family Reunification Act of 2001, 107th Congress, 1st Session, U.S. House of Representatives. Criticism of the bill by leading Republicans appears here: Julia Malone, "Push Is On to Relax Some Immigration Laws," *Atlanta J. & Const.* (May 16, 2002). In a letter to fellow Republicans opposing Frank's bill, Lamar Smith said, "It's hard to know where to begin a list of objections."
48. Immigration and Naturalization Service, *Statistical Yearbooks* (1996–2000).
49. See, Immigration and Naturalization Service, *Statistical Yearbooks* ch. 6 (2002–2003).
50. On the Patriot Act, see: Susan Akram and Kevin Johnson, "Race, Civil Rights, and Immigration Law after September 11, 2001: The Targeting of Arabs and Muslims," 58 *N.Y.U. Ann. Surv. Am. L.* 295 (2002); "U.S. Detention of Aliens in Aftermath of September 11 Attacks," 96 *Am. J. Int. L.* 470 (2002).

51. Mydans, supra note 45; and Paddock, supra note 46. See also, Deborah Sontag, "In a Homeland Far From Home," *N.Y. Times* (Nov. 16, 2003).
52. See, generally, Tien-Li Loke, "Trapped in Domestic Violence: The Impact of United States Immigration Laws on Battered Women," 6 *B.U. Pub. Int. L. J.* 589 (1997); and Janet Calvo, "The Violence Against Women Act: An Opportunity for the Justice Department to Confront Domestic Violence," 72 *Int. Releases* 485 (1995).
53. Pub. L. 103-322 (1994). VAWA appears in Title VI of the Act. Subsequent amendments to the Act can be found in Pub. L. 104–208, Pub. L. 105–119, Pub. L. 106–386, Pub. L. 107–273, and Pub. L. 108–21.
54. See: Linda Kelly, "Domestic Violence Survivors: Surviving the Beatings of 1996," 11 *Geo. Immigr. L. J.* 303 (1997); Michell Anderson, "A License to Abuse: The Impact of Conditional Status on Female Immigrants," 102 *Yale L. J.* 1401 (1993); and Elizabeth Shor, "Domestic Abuse and Alien Women in Immigration Law: Response and Responsibility," 9 *Cornell J.L. & Pub. Pol'y* 697 (2000).
55. Shor, supra note 54.
56. Christine McConville, "Cambodians Fear Deportation Plan," *Bost. Globe* (Nov. 14, 2002). For additional background on the Cambodian immigrant community in Lowell, see: Tuyet-Lan Pho and Anne Mulvey, "Southeast Asian Women in Lowell: Family Relations, Gender Roles, and Community Concerns," 24 *Frontiers* 101 (2003).
57. See Leslie, supra note 46; and Tram Nguyen, "Sent Back," *Colorlines* (Jan. 31, 2003).
58. Porthira Chhim, "Deportation Crisis," *Searac Bridge* (2001).
59. See, for example, Hearing of the Homeland Security Subcommittee in the House (Mar. 17, 2004); Hearing of the Homeland Security Subcommittee in the Senate (Mar. 30, 2004); Testimony of Timothy Danahey, National President of the Federal Law Enforcement Officers Association, to the House Subcommittee on Immigration, Border Security, and Claims (Mar. 11, 2004).

Chapter 5

1. Carlos Miranda, United States "Commission on Immigration Reform: The Interim and Final Reports," 38 *Santa Clara L. Rev.* 645, 666 (1998).
2. Testimony of Professor Barbara Jordan, Chair, U.S. Commission on Immigration Reform, to the House Subcommittee on Immigration and Claims (Jun. 28, 1995).
3. Miranda, supra note 1, 666-667. The Commission's report appears as: Commission on Immigration Reform, Legal Immigration: Setting Priorities (1995); Leiden's opinion appears in the Appendix.
4. Commission on Immigration Reform, supra note 3, Executive Summary.
5. Leiden, supra note 2.
6. Commission on Immigration Reform, U.S. Immigration Policy: Restoring Credibility (1994).
7. Testimony of Warren Leiden, Partner, Berry, Appleman, & Leiden, to the Senate Subcommittee on Immigration (Apr. 4, 2001).
8. For discussions of Proposition 187, immigrants, and the Welfare Act, see: Michael Scaperlanda, "Who Is My Neighbor? An Essay on Immigrants, Welfare Reform, and the Constitution," 29 *Conn. L. Rev.* 1587 (1997); Nora Demleitner, "The Fallacy of Social 'Citizenship,' or the Threat of Exclusion," 12 *Geo. Immigr. L. J.* 35 (1997); and Berta Hernandez-Truyol and Kimberly Johns, "Global Rights, Local Wrongs, and Legal Fixes: An International Human Rights Critique of Immigration and Welfare Reform," 71 *So. Cal. L. Rev.* 547 (1998). For a brief discussion of the political debates surrounding Proposition 187 and its political popularity in California, see John Park, "Race Discourse and Proposition 187," 2 *Mich. J. Race & L.* 175 (1996); and Kent Ono and John Sloop, *Shifting Borders: Rhetoric, Immigration, and California's Proposition* 187 (2002).
9. See, for example, George Borjas and S. Trejo, "Immigrant Participation in the Welfare System," 44 *Ind. & Lab. Rel. Rev.* 195 (1991); F. Blau, "The Use of Transfer Payments by Immigrants," 37 *Ind. & Lab. Rel. Rev.* 222 (1984); George Borjas and L. Hilton, "Immigration and the Welfare State: Immigrant Participation in Means-Tested Entitlement Programs," 111 *Quart. J. Econ.* 575 (1996). For a slightly different view, see M. Tienda and L. Jensen,

"Immigration and Public Assistance Participation: Dispelling the Myth of Dependency," 15 *Soc. Sci. Res.* 372 (1986). For key Congressional testimony leading up to the Welfare Act, see: Testimony of Stephen Moore, Director of Fiscal Policy Studies at the Cato Institute, to the House Subcommittee on Human Resources (Jan. 27, 1995); Testimony of David Stein, Executive Director for the Federation for American Immigration Reform, to the Senate Committee on Finance (Mar. 27, 1995); Testimony of Karen Narasaki, Executive Director for the National Asian Pacific American Legal Consortium, to the House Subcommittee on Immigration and Claims (Jun 29, 1995); Testimony of Jane Ross, Director of Income Security Issues in the Health, Education, and Human Services Division of the United States General Accounting Office, to the Senate Subcommittee on Immigration (Feb. 6, 1996); Testimony of Karen Darner, Virginia House of Delegates, on behalf of the National Conference of State Legislatures, to the Senate Committee on Finance (Mar. 12, 1996); Statement of Senator Pete Domenici to the Senate Budget Committee, Subcommittee on Federal Welfare Benefits for Immigrants (Mar. 12, 1996); Testimony of Mary Jo Bane, to the House Subcommittee on Human Resources (May 22, 1996); Testimony of Michael Fix, Jeffrey Passel, and Wendy Wassermann, to the House Subcommittee on Human Resources (May 23, 1996). Senator Pete Domenici mentioned specifically the scholarly work that had been published by Professor Borjas, which showed that "immigrants use welfare and social services at higher rates than the native population and for longer periods of time." Borjas' findings and methodology were criticized by Fix, Passel, and Wassermann, each of whom were leading researchers at the Urban Institute, a leading nonprofit research institute based in Washington D.C.

10. Ross, supra note 9. Similar figures and statistics were cited in Fix, Passel, and Wassermann, supra note 9, although these researchers insisted that rates of welfare use for non-citizens were only "slightly higher" than for citizens.

11. Pub. L. 104–193, §400. In its entirety, the section reads as follows: "The Congress makes the following statements concerning national policy with respect to welfare and immigration: (1) Self-sufficiency has been a basic principle of United States immigration law since this country's earliest immigration statutes. (2) It continues to be the immigration policy of the United States that—(A) aliens within the Nation's borders not depend on public resources to meet their needs, but rather rely on their own capabilities and the resources of their families, their sponsors, and private organizations, and (B) the availability of public benefits not constitute an incentive for immigration to the United States. (3) Despite the principle of self-sufficiency, aliens have been applying for and receiving public benefits from Federal, State, and local governments at increasing rates. (4) Current eligibility rules for public assistance and unenforceable financial support agreements have proved wholly incapable of assuring that individual aliens not burden the public benefits system. (5) It is a compelling government interest to enact new rules for eligibility and sponsorship agreements in order to assure that aliens be self-reliant in accordance with national immigration policy. (6) It is a compelling government interest to remove the incentive for illegal immigration provided by the availability of public benefits. (7) With respect to the State authority to make determinations concerning the eligibility of qualified aliens for public benefits in this title, a State that chooses to follow the Federal classification in determining the eligibility of such aliens for public assistance shall be considered to have chosen the least restrictive means available for achieving the compelling governmental interest of assuring that aliens be self-reliant in accordance with national immigration policy."

12. See generally, James Gimpel and James Edwards, *The Congressional Politics of Immigration Reform* (1999).

13. For a detailed discussion of the legislative debates preceding the immigration rules of 1996, see: David Reimers, *Unwelcome Strangers: American Identity and the Turn against Immigration* (1998).

14. Reimers, Supra note 13 (1998). See also: Linda Kelly, "Preserving the Right to Family Unity: Championing Notions of Social Contract and Community Ties in the Battle of Plenary Power Versus Aliens' Rights," 41 *Vill. L. Rev.* 725 (1996).

15. For a thorough review of welfare reform before and after the Clinton administration, see *Economic and Social Security and Substandard Working Conditions: The New World of Welfare* (Rebecca Blank and Ron Haskins, Eds., 2001).

16. Economic and Social Security, supra note 15 (Rebecca Blank and Ron Haskins, Eds., 2001), especially part I.

17. Pub. L. 104–193, at §101.

18. Pub. L. 104–193, at §101. For an interesting discussion of welfare policy and conceptions of family, particularly in relation to teen motherhood, see: Kristin Luker, *Dubious Conceptions: The Politics of Teenage Pregnancy* (1996); and *Race and the Politics of Welfare Reform* (Sanford Schram, Joe, Soss, and Richard Fording, Eds., 2003).

19. For problems with implementing "devolution," see Economic and Social Security, supra note 15, part III.

20. For a detailed discussion of this issue, see Michael Wishnie, "Laboratories of Bigotry? Devolution of the Immigration Power, Equal Protection, and Federalism," 76 *N.Y.U. L. Rev.* 493 (2001). Wishnie, at 496, explained: "The Welfare Act's authorization of state discrimination against immigrants was an attempt by Congress to devolve some of the exclusively federal immigration power to the states, and with it the substantial immunity from ordinary judicial scrutiny that long has accompanied exercises of the federal immigration power. Although this devolution is not explicit, I argue that it should be presumed because, under any other construction of the Welfare Act, the current rash of anti-immigrant state welfare rules are obviously invalid under *Graham's* settled rule that state welfare discrimination against legal immigrants is unconstitutional." See also, Graham v. Richardson, 403 U.S. 365 (1971).

21. Pub. L. 104–193, §431.

22. Pub. L. 104–193, §421. For a detailed discussion of the specific regulations promulgated to implement the Welfare Act, see Michael Sheridan, "The New Affidavit of Support and Other 1996 Amendments to Immigration and Welfare Provisions Designed to Prevent Aliens from Becoming Public Charges," 31 *Creighton L. R.* 741 (1998). For detailed overviews of the new rules in 1996 and their implications, see Thomas Espenshade, Jessica Baraka, and Gregory Huber, "Implications of the 1996 Welfare and Immigration Reform Acts for U.S. Immigration," 23 *Popul. & Dev. Rev.* 769 (1997).

23. Espenshade, Baraka, and Huber, supra note 22: "Approximately 500,000 non-citizen SSI and AFDC recipients [were] expected to lose eligibility by the fall of 1997, representing a caseload reduction of 35%. While most of those becoming ineligible are legal immigrants, some of the 200,000 refugee recipients are no longer eligible if they have been in the United States more than five years. Similarly, all of the approximately one million immigrants currently receiving food stamps and an additional 600,000 with full Medicaid coverage are expected to lose their benefits."

24. Espenshade, Baraka, and Huber, supra note 22. "SSI" refers to supplemental security income, which involve cash payments to eligible blind, aged, or disabled persons; "AFDC" refers to aid to families with dependent children, also a cash assistance program to eligible families with minor children.

25. Austin Fragomen, "Welfare Bill Severely Curtails Public Assistance to Non-Citizens," 30 *Int. Mig. Rev.* 1087, 1089, 1094 (1996).

26. Pub. L. 104–208, §531.

27. Pub. L. 104–208, at §551.

28. Pub. L. 104–208. "Upon notification that a sponsored alien has received any means-tested public benefit, the appropriate nongovernmental entity which provided such benefit or the appropriate entity of the Federal Government, a State, or any political subdivision of a State shall request reimbursement by the sponsor in an amount which is equal to the unreimbursed costs of such benefit." And, "Any person subject to the requirement of paragraph (1) who fails to satisfy such requirement shall, after notice and opportunity to be heard, be subject to a civil penalty of—(A) not less than $250 or more than $2,000, or (B) if such failure occurs with knowledge that the sponsored alien has received any means-tested public...not less than $2,000 or more than $5,000."

29. Pub. L. 104–208.

30. Maria Enchautegui and Aaron Sparrow, "Poverty among Long-Term U.S. Immigrants," (Report to the Urban Institute, 1997).

31. See, Joyce Vialet, "Immigration: The New Affidavit of Support—Questions, Answers, and Issues" 6 (Congressional Research Service, 97–1054 EPW, 1997), and Celia Dugger, "Immigrant Study Finds Many Below New Income Level," *N.Y. Times* (Mar. 16, 1997).

32. Testimony of Dan Stein, supra note 9.
33. The characterization of FAIR comes from Reimers, supra note 13, 37.
34. Testimony of Karen Narasaki, supra note 9. Narasaki's testimony indicated that major Asian American civil rights groups were mostly concerned about preserving welfare benefits for poorer Asian immigrants, preserving family reunification categories, and limiting the adverse impacts of a public discussion about immigration likely to spark violence against immigrants. Narasaki named other national Asian American organizations that shared these concerns, including: the Organization of Chinese Americans, the Japanese American Citizens' League, Chinese for Affirmative Action, the National Association for Korean Americans, the Asian Pacific American Labor Alliance, and the National Asian Pacific American Bar Association.
35. Bane, supra note 9. Along with Peter Edelman, another high-ranking official in the Department of Health and Human Services, Professor Bane subsequently resigned her post in a very public protest against the President's signing of the Welfare Act in 1996. Mr. Edelman cited the likely harm of the Act on poorer American children; Professor Bane only cited "deep concerns about the [Act]." Neither cited harm to immigrants as a leading reason for their resignations. See, Barbara Vobejda and Judith Havemann, "2 HHS Officials Quit Over Welfare Changes," Wash. Post (Sep. 12, 1996).
36. Darner, supra note 9.
37. Coverage of organized political protests about immigrant welfare access was extensive in 1997, and the following articles are representative of this phenomenon only: Jean Hopfensperger, "Hmong Immigrants' Tearful Testimony Underscores State's Welfare Struggle," Star Trib. (Jan. 31, 1997); Harriet Chiang, "Two-Fisted Counterpunch to Welfare Law: First Class-Action Suits Filed in New York, San Francisco," S.F. Chron. (Mar. 27, 1997); Pamela Constable, "Legal Immigrants Pulling Together to Protest Threats to Their Benefits," Wash. Post (Apr. 14, 1997); Pamela Constable, "Laotian Veterans Join Fight for Benefits," Wash. Post (May 8, 1997); Judith Haveman, 'Republicans Start to Break Ranks on Welfare Cutoff for Legal Immigrants," Wash. Post (Apr. 20, 1997); and Gregg Aamot, 'Hmong Putting American Politics to Work for Them," Star Trib. (Aug. 18, 1997).
38. Hopfensperger, supra note 37.
39. Constable, Laotian Veterans, supra note 37.
40. Chiang, supra note 37.
41. Constable, Legal Immigrants, supra note 37.
42. Haveman, supra note 37. Delegate Karen Darner of Virginia had warned of this result in her testimony to Congress a year earlier; see Darner, supra note 9.
43. On Southeast Asian poverty, see generally, Eric Tang, Southeast Asian Poverty in the United States, 18 Social Text 55 (2000). At 55, Tang wrote: "Southeast Asians in the United States—primarily Vietnamese, Lao, Hmong, and Cambodian immigrants—represent the largest per capita race or ethnic group in the country receiving public assistance. Originally placed on federal welfare rolls as a temporary and 'adaptive' measure under the Indochina Migration and Refugee Assistance Act of 1975, a large segment of Southeast Asian refugees who fled their homelands in the aftermath of the U.S. invasion of Vietnam and the subsequent bombing of Cambodia by the United States are now entering a third consecutive decade of welfare dependency, contrary to government officials' predictions of a seamless transition into American labor markets. Stripped of their refugee status in the post-Cold War era, virtually all Southeast Asians have now been reclassified as permanent residents (or 'legal' immigrants) and are therefore subject to the impending cuts under the [Welfare Act]. The consequences of the new laws' 'immigrant removal' campaign are sweeping and disastrous for Southeast Asian communities that, in California alone, have shown poverty and welfare dependency rates of nearly 80 percent for the state's entire Southeast Asian population." His estimates were drawn from Ngoan Le, "Policy for a Community 'at-Risk,'" in The State of Asian Pacific America: Policy Issues to the Year 2020 (Don Nakanishi, Ed., 1993).
44. Non-Citizen Benefit Clarification Act of 1998, Pub. L. 105–306, §2; and also, the Balanced Budget Act of 1997, Pub. L. 105-33.
45. George Borjas, "Welfare Reform and Immigrant Participation in Welfare Programs," 36 Int. Migr. Rev. 1093, 1101–1102, 1112 (2002). At 1121, Professor Borjas suggested that this was a counterintuitive trend: "In 1996, Congress gave individual states the option to supplement the federal benefits available to immigrants with state-provided benefits. It turned out that

almost all of the states with large immigrant populations chose to extend the state-provided safety nets to immigrant households. The political choices made by these states prevented many immigrant households from being removed from the welfare rolls, and helped attenuate the impact of welfare reform on immigrant welfare use.... From an economic perspective, the responses made by the states with large immigrant populations seem puzzling. One could easily have argued that once Congress gave states the opportunity to choose state-specific policies, many of the states most affected by immigration would have chosen to discourage welfare use by immigrants residing within their borders—rather than pursue policies that further encouraged welfare use."

46. George Borjas, "Welfare Reform and Immigrant Participation in Welfare Programs," 36 *Int. Migr. Rev.* 1093, 1101–1102, 1112 (2002).

47. *Id.*

48. For studies that explore this question, see: Fred Arnold, Benjamin Carino, James Fawcett, and Insook Park, "Estimating the Immigration Multiplier: An Analysis of Recent Korean and Filipino Immigration to the United States," 23 *Int. Mig. Rev.* 813 (1989); Frank Bean, G. Vernez, and C. Keely, *Opening and Closing the Doors: Evaluating Immigration Reform and Control* (1989); Thanh Tran, "Sponsorship and Employment Status Among Indochinese Refugees in the United States," 25 *Int. Mig. Rev.* 536 (1991); Jennifer Glick, Frank Bean, and Jennifer Van Hook, "Immigration and Changing Patterns of Extended Family Household Structure in the United States, 1970–1990," 59 *J. Marriage & Fam.* 177 (1997); and *The New Americans: Economic, Demographic, and Fiscal Effects of Immigration* (James Smith and Barry Edmonston, Eds., 1997).

49. One innovative study attempts to develop a methodological approach to this type of research question. See: Guellermina Jasso, Douglas Massey, Mark Rosenzweig, and James Smith, "The New Immigrant Survey Pilot (NIS-P): Overview and New Findings about U.S. Legal Immigrants at Admission," 37 *Demography* 127 (2000).

50. United States Department of Homeland Security, Office of Immigration Statistics, 2002 Yearbook of Immigration Statistics Table 5 (2003).

51. *Id.*

52. See, for example, Ann Simmons, "Lawsuit Filed over Immigrant Medical Costs," *Los Angeles Times* (Aug. 17, 2004).

Chapter 6

1. The quote and the relevant sections of the Exclusion Act governing non-immigrants are in Low Yam Chow, 13 F. 605, 609-611 (Cir.Ct.D.CA. 1882).

2. Ernesto Galaraza, *Merchants of Labor: The Mexican Bracero Story* (1964); Juan Ramon Garcia, *Operation Wetback: The Mass Deportation of Mexican Undocumented Workers in 1954* (1980), and Kitty Calavita, *Inside the State: The Bracero Program, Immigration, and the I.N.S.* (1992). For contemporary discussions of the Bracero Program, or Bracero-like programs, see Michael Olivas, "The Chronicles, My Grandfather's Stories, and Immigration Law: The Slave Traders Chronicle as Racial History," 34 *St. Louis U.L.J.* 425 (1990), and Christopher Cameron, "Borderline Decisions: *Hoffman Plastic Compounds*, the New Bracero Program, and the Supreme Court's Role in Making Federal Labor Policy," 51 *UCLA L. Rev. 1* (2003).

3. See Cameron, supra note 2.

4. See generally, Keith Crane, Beth Asch, Joanna Heilbrunn, and Danielle Cullinane, *The Effect of Employer Sanctions on the Flow of Undocumented Immigrants to the United States* (1990); Michael Fix and Paul Hill, *Enforcing Employer Sanctions: Challenges and Strategies* (1990). Government reports stated similar findings; for examples, see: United States Department of Labor, Employer Sanctions and U.S. Labor Markets: Second Report (1991); and United States Department of Labor, Impact of IRCA on the U.S. Labor Market and Economy (1991). For estimates of the population of illegal Chinese immigrants, see Peter Kwong, *Forbidden Workers: Illegal Chinese Immigrants and American Labor* (1999). For a succinct discussion of undocumented migration, its history, and some of the difficulties inherent in measuring the population, see Thomas Espenshade, "Unauthorized Immigration to the United States," 21 *Ann. Rev. Soc.* 194 (1995).

5. Enid Trucios-Haynes, "Temporary Workers and Future Immigration Policy Conflicts: Protecting U.S. Workers and Satisfying Demands for Global Human Capital," 40 *Brandeis L. J.* 967, 991 (2002).
6. Pub. L. 101-238, §2.
7. Pub. L. 101-238, §3(b).
8. Trucios-Haynes, supra note 5.
9. INA § 214(i)(1) (1998). The relevant portions of the Immigration Act of 1990 are found in Pub. L. 101–649 §205(c)(2).
10. Pub. L. 101–649 §205(c)(2)(C).
11. Pub. L. 101–649, §205(c)(2)(D). The penalties are outlined in the subsequent section, including a $1,000 fine for each attempted hiring of a non-immigrant in contravention of these procedures.
12. Pub. L. 101–649, §205(a).
13. See Pub. L. 101–649, §205(b). For a discussion of the dual intent rule, see: Susan Martin, B. Lindsay Lowell, and Philip Martin, "U.S. Immigration Policy: Admission of High Skilled Workers," 16 *Geo. Immigr. L. J.* 619 (2002); and Margaret Usdansky and Thomas Espenshade, "The H-1B in Historical Perspective: The Evolution of U.S. Policy Toward Foreign-Born Workers" (Center for Comparative Immigration Studies, Working Paper, May 2000).
14. For a review of the process, see Brian Halliday, "In Order to Hire the Best Person for the Job, We Have to Do What?: A Look at the H-1B Visa Program," 11 *J. Law. & Pub. Pol'y* 33 (1999). The process had to be diagrammed for Congressional leaders in a report by the General Accounting Office: United States General Accounting Office, H-1B Foreign Workers: Better Controls Needed To Help Employers and Protect Workers, GAO/HEHS-00-157 (2000).
15. General Accounting Office: supra note 14 (2000), §207 (O).
16. See SY 2001, Table 38. Persons from Europe accounted for 58% of the total number of O visas, Asians accounted for about 14%.
17. See SY 2001, Table 38, §207 (P).
18. See 65 Interpreter Rel. 710 (1988).
19. See, for example, Stephen Legomsky, *Immigration Law and Policy* 255 (1992).
20. See Martin, Lowell, and Martin, supra note 12, 629. See also, U.S. Immigration and Naturalization Service, Leading Employers of Specialty Occupation Workers (H-1B): October 1999 to February 2000 (June 2000); U.S. Immigration and Naturalization Service, Report on Characteristics of Specialty Occupation Workers (H-1B): Fiscal Year 2000 (April 2002); U.S. Immigration and Naturalization Service, Report on Characteristics of Specialty Occupation Workers (H-1B): Fiscal Year 2001 (July 2002);
21. Pub. L. 105-277.
22. Pub. L. 105-277, §411.
23. Statement of Orrin Hatch, Chairman of the Senate Judiciary Committee, to the Senate Judiciary Committee (Feb. 25, 1998).
24. Testimony of Kenneth Alvarez, Vice President of Human Resources, Sun Microsystems, to the Senate Judiciary Committee (Feb. 25, 1998); Testimony of Michael Murray, Vice President of Resources and Administration, Microsoft Corporation, to the Senate Judiciary Committee (Feb. 25, 1998); Testimony of T.J. Rodgers, President and CEO of Cypress Semiconductor Corporation, to the Senate Judiciary Committee (Feb. 25, 1998); and Testimony of Stephen Director, Dean of the College of Engineering, University of Michigan, to the Senate Judiciary Committee (Feb. 25, 1998).
25. For an overview of the high-tech firms favoring the increased cap, see Carla Marinucci and John Wildermuth, "Silicon Valley CEOs Flex Political Muscle," *S.F. Chron.* (3 Oct 1998). For a useful review of the public debates around the ACWIA, see Jung Haim, "American Competitiveness and Workforce Improvement Act of 1998: Balancing Economic and Labor Interests Under the New H-1B Visa Program," 85 *Cornell L. Rev.* 1673 (2000); and Constantine Potamianos, "The Temporary Admission of Skilled Workers to the United States under the H-1B Program: Economic Boon or Domestic Work Force Scourge?" 11 *Geo. Immigr. L.J.* 789 (1997).
26. Alvarez, supra note 24.
27. See Rodgers, supra note 24, and Miller, supra note 24.
28. Alvarez, supra note 24.

29. Rodgers, supra note 24.
30. Media coverage of the H-1B has been extensive. Useful summaries can be found in: Wayne Cornelius and Thomas Espenshade, "The International Migration of the Highly Skilled: 'High Tech Braceros' in the Global Labor Market," and B. Lindsay Lowell, "The Foreign Temporary Workforce and Shortages in Information Technology," both in *The International Migration of the Highly Skilled: Demand, Supply, and Development Consequences in Sending and Receiving Countries* (Wayne Cornelius, Thomas Espenshade, and Idean Salehyan, Eds., 2001).
31. Murray, supra note 24.
32. Alvarez, supra note 24.
33. Murray, supra note 24.
34. See, for example, an amusing account in James Wallace, *Hard Drive: Bill Gates and the Making of the Microsoft Empire* (1993).
35. Testimony of Robert Lerman, Director of Human Resources Policy, Urban Institute, to the Senate Judiciary Committee (Feb. 25, 1998).
36. The IEEE produces several dozen publications in electrical engineering, computer science, and related fields, and it awards several professional citations for people making an exceptional contribution to these fields. It is one of the most respected professional organizations in engineering.
37. Testimony of John Reinert, President of the Institute of Electrical and Electronics Engineers, to the Senate Judiciary Committee (Feb. 25, 1998). Reinhart said: "IEEE-USA favors employment-based admissions policies that permit employers to hire foreign professionals, including engineers and computer specialists, based on a verifiable lack of appropriately skilled or easily trainable American workers—not simply because it is easier or less expensive to hire foreign workers who may be willing to accept less than prevailing wages in order to enter or remain in the United States. A lack of effective investigatory and enforcement provisions under current law exacerbate the potential for abuses under the H-1B temporary admissions program." Scholarly work on this issue has produced interesting findings. For instance, consider this report from Thomas Espenshade, Margaret Usdansky, and Chang Chung, "Employment and Earnings of Foreign-Born Scientists and Engineers," 20 *Pop. Res. & Pol'y Rev.* 81, 101–102 (2001): "Foreign-born [scientists and engineers] earn more per year on average than do the native born. In our sample of [scientists and engineers] who worked full-time and full-year in the calendar year preceding data collection, the foreign born had a wage advantage over natives of 6.1 percent in 1989 and 2.1 percent in 1996. These gaps are explained primarily by the fact that the foreign born have more years of schooling than natives and that they were more likely than natives to live in large metropolitan areas with a higher cost of living. When these and other demographic and socioeconomic factors are held constant, immigrant [scientists and engineers] earned 4.4 percent less than comparable natives in 1989 and 9.3 percent in 1996."
38. The parallel appeared often in congressional testimony and in media accounts, as well as in the scholarly literature. See, for example: Gaiutra Bahadur, "India's High-Tech Braceros: 'New Economy' Migrant Workers," *Austin-Amer. Statesman* (Nov. 19, 2000); and Cornelius and Espenshade, supra note 30.
39. Testimony of Norman Matloff, Professor of Computer Science, University of California at Davis, to the House Judiciary Committee (Apr. 21, 1998).
40. See, for example, INS SY 2001, Table 5, and B. Lindsay Lowell, H-1B "Temporary Workers: Estimating the Population" (Working Paper, Center for Comparative Immigration Studies, 2000). See also, Thomas Espenshade, "High-End Immigrants and the Shortage of Skilled Labor," 20 *Pop. Res. & Pol'y Rev.* 135 (2001).
41. The phrase comes from the title of a critical report, published by a well established organization in favor of more restrictive immigration policies in general: Federation for American Immigration Reform, *Deleting American Workers: Abuse of the Temporary Foreign Worker System in the High Tech Industry* (2003).
42. For background on the legislative debates in immigration policy, see James Gimpel and James Edwards, *The Congressional Politics of Immigration Reform* (1999).
43. One subsequent report summarizes these efforts. See, United States General Accounting Office, H-1B Foreign Workers: Better Tracking Needed to Help Determine H-1B Program's Effects on U.S. Workforce, GAO-03-883 (2003). This report stated that many issues were

still unresolved or ambiguous, as in id., 4: "The majority of employers interviewed [for this GAO study] cited cost and lengthy petition processing times as major disadvantages to hiring H-1B workers; however, they said they would continue to use the H-1B program to find candidates with the skills needed. Some employers said that they hired H-1B workers in part because these workers would often accept lower salaries than similarly qualified U.S. workers; however, these employers said they never paid H-1B workers less than the required wage. [The Department of] Labor is responsible for, among other things, ensuring that employers do not violate H-1B wage agreements, and continues to find instances of employers not paying H-1B workers the wage required by law; however, the extent to which such violations occur is unknown and may be due in part to Labor's limited investigative authority."

44. Pub. L. 105–277, §414.
45. Pub. L. 105–277, at §§412 and 413. "The term 'H-1B-dependent employer means an employer that—(i)(I) has 25 or fewer full-time equivalent employees who are employed in the United States; and (II) employs more than 7 H-1B non-immigrants; (ii)(I) has at least 26 but not more than 50 full-time equivalent employees who are employed in the United States; and (II) employs more than 12 H-1B non-immigrants; or (iii)(I) has at least 51 full-time equivalent employees who are employed in the United States; and (II) employs H-1B non-immigrants in a number that is equal to at least 15 percent of the number of such full-time equivalent employees."
46. Pub. L. 105–277, §413.

Chapter 7

1. Senate Report 106–260 (Apr. 11, 2000). The Report continued: "Demetrios G. Papademetriou, co-director of the International Migration Policy Program at the Carnegie Endowment for International Peace, wrote this year, 'While we are again showing how not to have the right conversation about foreign-born high-tech workers, people who come into this country on H-1B visas, the rest of the developed world is waking up to the fact that America's cherry-picking of international tech talent amounts to an enormous competitive advantage, one that, if left unchallenged, could extend U.S. dominance in information technology indefinitely. Our competitors are doing something about it. Germany, Canada, the United Kingdom, and Australia, among others, have already entered the sweepstakes for high-tech workers.' … The question is simple: Will America choose to remain a global leader in crucial academic, science and technology fields?"
2. Viji Sundaram, "Immigrant Support Network: Lobbying Successfully for New High-Tech Bill," *India West* (Nov. 10, 2000).
3. Pete Carey, "Foreign Workers Form Network to Lobby Congress for Relief," *San Jose Mercury News* (Nov. 19, 2000). For a helpful discussion of the Immigrants Support Network, see: Alan Hyde, "Employee Organization in Silicon Valley: Networks, Ethnic Organizations, and New Unions," 4 *U. Pa. J. Lab. & Emp. L.* 493 (2002). For a thorough review of how H-1B rules were harmful to the position of foreign workers, see: Sabrina Underwood, "Achieving the American Daydream: The Social, Economic, and Political Inequalities Experienced by Temporary Workers Under the H-1B Visa Program," 15 *Geo. Immigr. L. J.* 727 (2001).
4. See, for example, Julie Watts, "The H-1B Visa: Free Market Solutions for Business and Labor," 20 *Pop. Res. & Pol'y Rev.* 143 (2001). For a helpful discussion of labor unions and immigration policy, see: Leah Haus, "Openings in the Wall: Transnational Migrants, Labor Unions, and U.S. Immigration Policy," 49 *Int. Org.* 285 (1995).
5. Immigration and Naturalization Service, *2001 Statistical Yearbook* (2002).
6. See Additional Views of Senators Leahy, Kennedy, Biden, Feingold, Torricelli, and Schumer, appended to Senate Report 106-260 (Apr. 11, 2000).
7. Stuart Anderson, "Wide-Spread Abuse of H-1Bs and Employment-Based Immigration? The Evidence Says Otherwise," 73 *Interpreter Rel.* 637, 650 (1996); see also, "Survey and Analysis of H-1B Labor Condition Application Decisions," 72 *Interpreter Rel.* 51 (1995).
8. See, for example: Mark McDonald, "Demand for H-1B Visas Spawns Fraud, Abuse in India," *San Jose Mercury News* (Nov. 20, 2000); Pete Carey, "New Rules Ease Worker Short-

age, but Fraud and Abuse Remain," *San Jose Mercury News* (Nov. 18, 2000); and Aziz Haniffa, "'Body Shopping' Being Played Up by Anti-H-1B Lobby," *India Abroad* (Feb. 4, 2000).

9. United States General Accounting Office, "H-1B Foreign Workers: Better Tracking Needed to Help Determine H-1B Program's Effects on U.S. Workforce," *GAO-03-883* (2003). See, for example, the comment on pages 5 and 6: "INS is responsible for ensuring that H-1B positions are in fact specialty occupations and that workers granted entry are qualified for those positions. Until recently, INS had no national systemic approach for adjudicators to follow to ensure the consistent review of employer petitions. Further, INS staff conducting these reviews continued to lack easy access to specific, case-related information that would help them assess the merit of employers' requests, which can also lead to incorrect approvals of requests. Because existing supervisory review and performance appraisal systems for INS staff reviewing petitions are based on the number of requests processed, rather than the quality of the review, staff can be rewarded for handling of petitions rather than for careful scrutiny of petitions' merits. As a result, there is not sufficient assurance that INS reviews are adequate for detecting program noncompliance or abuse. In addition, INS decisions about the priority of H-1B application processing related to other types of petitions handled by INS have resulted in delays of several months to process employers' requests for H-1B workers." The GAO recommended several changes to the handling of H-1B applications. "INS generally did not agree with our recommendation, believing the current program procedures are sufficient to detect noncompliance and abuse. We continue to believe that actions beyond those taken by INS are warranted."

10. Robin Iredale, "The Internationalization of Professionals and the Assessment of Skills: Australia, Canada, and the U.S.," 16 *Geo. Immigr. L. J.* 797, 813 (2003).

11. The quotes are from AnnaLee Saxenian, "Silicon Valley's New Immigrant Entrepreneurs," in *The International Migration of the Highly Skilled: Demand, Supply, and Development Consequences in Sending and Receiving Countries* 197 (Wayne Cornelius, Thomas Espenshade, and Idean Salehyan, Eds., 2001). Professor Saxenian drew from an earlier study commissioned by the National Science Foundation: Jean Johnson and Mark Regets, International Mobility of Scientists and Engineers in the United States — Brain Drain or Brain Circulation? (*NSF Issue Brief* 98-316). See also, Henry Arthurs, "Reinventing Labor Law for the Global Economy," 22 *Berkeley J. Emp. & Lab. L.* 271 (2001), for a helpful discussion on managing transnational business networks and both low-end and high-end immigrants. For a useful discussion of employment versus other motives for permanent migration, see Ann Bagchi, "Migrant Networks and the Immigrant Professional: An Analysis of the Role of Weak Ties," 20 *Pop. Res. & Pol'y Rev.* 9 (2001).

12. Saxenian, supra note 11, 197: "And advances in transportation and communications technologies mean that even when these skilled immigrants choose not to return home, they still play a critical role as middlemen linking businesses in the United States to those in geographically distant regions." For a provocative study discussing "place" within an increasingly global context, see Manuel Castells, *The Rise of the Network Society* (2nd ed., 2000).

13. Testimony of Paul Kostek, president of the Institute of Electrical and Electronics Engineers—USA, to the House Subcommittee on Immigration and Claims (Aug. 5, 1999).

14. Testimony of David Smith, Director of Policy of the AFL-CIO, to the House Subcommittee on Immigration (Aug. 5, 1999). See also, testimony of Frank Brehm, Northwest Regional Coordinator for the Programmers' Guild, to the House Subcommittee on Immigration (May 25, 2000): "According to the Department of Labor, there is no credible evidence of a shortage of high-technology workers."

15. Statement of Lamar Smith, in the House Subcommittee on Immigration (Apr. 12, 2000). Scholars have since warned of the problems with raising the cap, as the negative consequences of increasing the cap might begin to outweigh the positive consequences for the American economy. For example, see B. Lindsay Lowell, "Skilled Temporary and Permanent Immigrants in the United States," 20 *Pop. Res. & Pol'y Rev.* 33, 55 (2001): "If Congress continues to raise the number of temporary workers permitted to work in the United States it is quite possible that we will witness an increase in what now appears to be isolated cases of abuse. Wage impacts may become notable. However, the evidence is yet to be systemically and convincingly marshaled to convince a large share of the policymaking audience that something currently is amiss. Rather, temporary workers are widely seen as playing a positive role in the US economy."

16. Pub. L. 106–313, §102.
17. Enid Trucios-Haynes, "Temporary Workers and Future Immigration Policy Conflicts: Protecting U.S. Workers and Satisfying Demands for Global Human Capital," 40 *Brandeis L. J.* 967, 1010 (2002).
18. Pub. L. 106–313, §105. For a helpful discussion of this provision and other changes to the H-1B visa under AC21, see "Looking to the North While Playing Doctor: Solving the H-1B Visa Problem by Following Canada's Lead," 10 *Minn. J. Global Trade* 433 (2001).
19. Pub. L. 106–313, §106(b).
20. U.S. Immigration and Naturalization Service, Report on H-1B Petitions, Third Quarter, Fiscal Year 2001, Table 1 (Aug. 2002).
21. One can find Professor Matloff's own biographical sketch on his web-site: http://heather.cs.ucdavis.edu/matloff.html. Professor Matloff made repeated references to these facts in congressional testimony.
22. Chae Chan Ping v. United States, 130 U.S. 581, 595 (1889).
23. Immigration and Naturalization Service, *2001 Statistical Yearbook* Table 10 (2002), and B. Lindsay Lowell, "Skilled Temporary and Permanent Immigrants in the United States," 20 *Pop. Res. & Pol'y Rev.* 33, 49 (2001).
24. Immigration and Naturalization Service, supra note 23.

Chapter 8

1. Elisabeth Bumiller, "Bush Would Give Illegal Workers Broad New Rights," *N.Y. Times* (Jan. 7, 2004).
2. Richard Stevenson and Steven Greenhouse, "Plan for Illegal Immigrant Workers Draws Fire From Two Sides," *N.Y. Times* (Jan. 8, 2004). See also: H.G. Reza, 'Despite Concerns, Guest Worker Idea Isn't Fueling a Surge to U.S." *L.A. Times* (Feb. 15, 2004).
3. Alan Zarembo, "Garment Workers Say Bush Guest Worker Plan Is an Ill Fit," *L.A. Times* (Feb. 8, 2004); and Leonel Sanchez, "Latinos Split on Bush's Immigration Plan, Citing Repatriation Provision," *San Diego Union Trib.* (Jan. 30, 2004).
4. See generally, Jospeh Nevins and Mike Davis, *Operation Gatekeeper: The Rise of the 'Illegal Alien' and the Remaking of the U.S.-Mexico Border* (2001); Edna Bonacich and Richard Appelbaum, *Behind the Label: Inequality in the Los Angeles Apparel Industry* (2000); and Daniel Rothenberg, *With these Hands: The Hidden World of Migrant Farmworkers Today* (2000).
5. See, Bill Myers, "Congress Lets H-1B Visa Program Revert to Original, Tighter Quota," *Chicago Daily L. Bull.* (Oct. 1, 2003).
6. Carrie Kirby, "Visa's Use Provokes Opposition By Techies: L-1 Regarded as Threat to Workers," *S.F. Chron.* (May 25, 2003); Katie Hafner and Daniel Preysman, "Special Visa's Use for Tech Workers Is Challenged," *N.Y. Times* (May 30, 2003); Ted Sickinger, "Clamor Rises Against Work Visas," *Oregonian* (Oct. 13, 2003); and Carolyn Lochhead, "Feinstein Seeking Changes in Skilled Worker Visa," *S.F. Chron.* (Jul, 30, 2003).
7. See, generally, President's Commission on Immigration Reform, Legal Immigration: Setting Priorities (1995).
8. United States Citizenship and Immigration Services, Naturalizations 2 (2003).
9. United States Citizenship and Immigration Services, Naturalizations, 2–3.
10. See, generally, "The Functionality of Citizenship," 110 *Harv. L. Rev.* 1814 (1997), citing Sally Jacobs, "U.S. Eases Rules for Immigrants with Disabilities," *Bost. Globe* (Mar. 19, 1997), and Teresa Mears, "Fears for Benefits Spur Rush for U.S. Citizenship," *Bost. Globe* (Mar. 11, 1997).
11. Bill Ong Hing, "Deported for Shoplifting?" *Wash. Post* (Dec. 29, 2002), reminds us that Wynona Ryder — convicted of a very significant amount of shoplifting — was lucky not to be an immigrant.
12. United States Citizenship and Immigration Services, supra note 8, 1.
13. The Act of 1952 also abolished finally the race-based criteria governing naturalization: after this, Asians were no longer "aliens ineligible for citizenship."

Index